Cambridge Primary

Computing

Learner's Book 2

Roland Birbal
Carissa Gookool
Michelle Koon Koon
Nazreen Mohammed
Michele Taylor

Series editor:
Roland Birbal

HODDER
EDUCATION
AN HACHETTE UK COMPANY

Although every effort has been made to ensure that website addresses are correct at time of going to press, Hodder Education cannot be held responsible for the content of any website mentioned in this book. It is sometimes possible to find a relocated web page by typing in the address of the home page for a website in the URL window of your browser.

Hachette UK's policy is to use papers that are natural, renewable and recyclable products and made from wood grown in well-managed forests and other controlled sources. The logging and manufacturing processes are expected to conform to the environmental regulations of the country of origin.

Orders: please contact Hachette UK Distribution, Hely Hutchinson Centre, Milton Road, Didcot, Oxfordshire, OX11 7HH. Telephone: +44 (0)1235 827827. Email education@hachette.co.uk. Lines are open from 9 a.m. to 5 p.m., Monday to Saturday, with a 24-hour message-answering service. You can also order through our website: www.hoddereducation.com

© Roland Birbal, Carissa Gookool, Michelle Koon Koon, Nazreen Mohammed, Michele Taylor 2023

First published in 2023 by
Hodder Education
An Hachette UK Company
Carmelite House
50 Victoria Embankment
London EC4Y 0DZ

www.hoddereducation.com

Impression number   10 9 8 7 6 5 4 3 2 1
Year   2027 2026 2025 2024 2023

Cover illustration by Lisa Hunt from Bright Agency
Illustrations by Vian Oelofsen, Stéphan Theron
Typeset in FS Albert 17/19 by IO Publishing CC
Produced by DZS Grafik, Printed in Slovenia

A catalogue record for this title is available from the British Library.
ISBN: 9781398368576

Contents

How to use this book

Get started! Talk about the new topic with a partner or small group.

Get started!
Look at the following instructions. They are for the game 'Simon says'.
1 Which instructions are clear?
2 What is missing in the instructions?

❶	Simon says, "Move 4 steps forward"
❷	Simon says, "Move"
❸	Simon says, "Run"
❹	Simon says, "Clap your hands two times"
❺	Simon says, "Run to the tree"

You will learn: A list of things you will learn in the unit.

You will learn:
* that an algorithm is a precise set of instructions
* that programs tell computers what to do
* how to write programs from algorithms.

In this unit, you will learn about algorithms and programs.

Warm up

You will need a sheet of paper. Follow the instructions below.
1 Draw a rectangle.
2 Draw a triangle over the rectangle.
3 In the rectangle, draw three small squares.
    * Show your drawing to your classmates.
    * Do your pictures look different?
The instructions are to draw an object. Your teacher will show you.
Talk in groups. Why are some people's drawings different?

Warm up: An offline activity to start your learning.

Do you remember?

Before starting this unit, check that you:
* know what an algorithm is
* can follow an algorithm
* know that the order of instructions is important
* know that algorithms are used to write code.

In this unit, you will use ScratchJr. There is an online chapter all about ScratchJr.

Do you remember? A list of things you should know before you start the unit.

Learn

Computer devices look different. However, they are all made from hardware and software.

Hardware

Hardware are the physical objects that make up a computing device. Here are some examples of hardware:

This processor is hardware. It is hidden inside all computing devices. You cannot see it, but a computing device cannot work without it.

Mia uses a keyboard to write a letter to her friend on the computer. The keyboard is hardware.

Zhu can use headphones to listen to music on her smartphone. Headphones are hardware.

Learn: Learn new computing skills with your teacher. Look at the instructions to help you.

Practise: Answer questions to learn more and practice your new skills.

Practise

For these questions, use the website your teacher gives you.

1 Use data from the table to make a bar graph.

Name	Favourite fruit
Zara	Banana
Viti	Banana
David	Orange
Jack	Orange
Annay	Orange
Sara	Banana
Liam	Apple

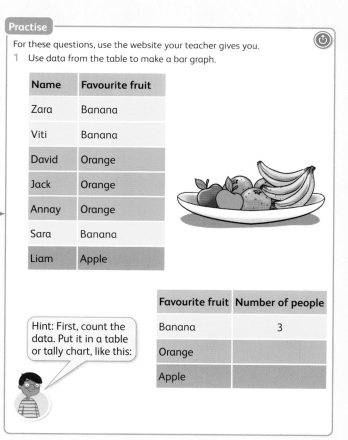

Hint: First, count the data. Put it in a table or tally chart, like this:

Favourite fruit	Number of people
Banana	3
Orange	
Apple	

Go further:
Activities to make you think carefully about computing.

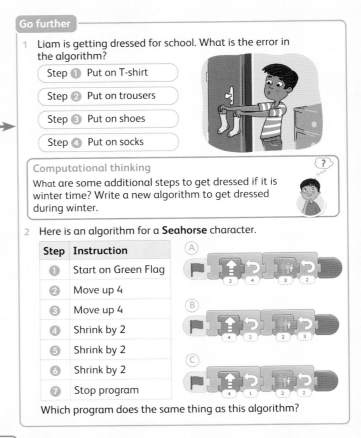

Go further

1 Liam is getting dressed for school. What is the error in the algorithm?

Step 1 Put on T-shirt

Step 2 Put on trousers

Step 3 Put on shoes

Step 4 Put on socks

Computational thinking

What are some additional steps to get dressed if it is winter time? Write a new algorithm to get dressed during winter.

2 Here is an algorithm for a **Seahorse** character.

Step	Instruction
1	Start on Green Flag
2	Move up 4
3	Move up 4
4	Shrink by 2
5	Shrink by 2
6	Shrink by 2
7	Stop program

Which program does the same thing as this algorithm?

Challenge yourself!

1 Start a new project. Add the correct code from the **Go further** activity to the **Seahorse** character.
2 Add a **Fish** character.
3 Create a program for the **Fish** to match this algorithm.

Step	Instruction
1	Start on Green Flag
2	Say "Hi Seahorse"
3	Move right (6)
4	Move left (2)
5	Play Pop sound
6	Repeat steps 3 to 5 two more times
7	Stop program

Test your code to see if you get the correct results.

4 Add the **Starfish** character to your project.
5 Add the code below to the **Starfish** and run it.

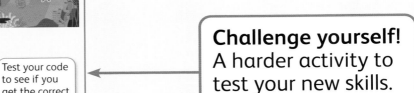

6 Change the code for the **Starfish** so it uses the **Repeat** block. The new code should get the same results.
7 Run your final program.

Challenge yourself!
A harder activity to test your new skills.

All links to additional resources can be found at: https://www.hoddereducation.co.uk/cambridgeextras

My project

1 Look at the algorithm to get out of a maze. It has one error. What is the error? How would you correct it?

Algorithm
Move right (2)
Move up (3)
Move right (4)
Move up (1)

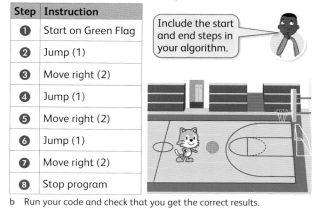

2 Think about the things you do every night when you go to bed. Write an algorithm for going to bed. Include all the things you do in the correct order.

3 a Create a program from the algorithm below for the **Basketball** character. Use the **Repeat** block.

Step	Instruction
❶	Start on Green Flag
❷	Jump (1)
❸	Move right (2)
❹	Jump (1)
❺	Move right (2)
❻	Jump (1)
❼	Move right (2)
❽	Stop program

Include the start and end steps in your algorithm.

   b Run your code and check that you get the correct results.

My project: A longer activity at the end of the unit to test the skills you have learnt so far.

Did you know?

The **Mars Climate Orbiter** was a spaceship.

A bug in the program controlling the spaceship caused an error. The mission could not be completed!

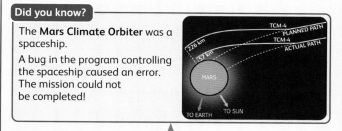

Did you know? Learn about interesting facts and information.

What can you do? Find out how much you have learnt and what you can do.

What can you do?

Read and review what you can do.

✔ I can find and correct errors in algorithms.

✔ I can identify the steps to perform tasks.

✔ I can create programs that use the repeat command.

Good job! Now you can create algorithms and programs that repeat instructions.

Computational thinking

Complete the algorithm in the table below with the steps to get the mouse to the cheese.

Step	Instruction
❶	Move right _____
❷	Move _____
❸	Move _____
❹	Move _____ (2)

Computational thinking: A task that tests your computational thinking skills.

Keywords

output: the results of an algorithm

input: the data that is given to an algorithm

Keywords: Understand new computing words. The **Glossary** at the end of the book also lists all of these words.

Giving instructions

Get started!

Look at the following instructions. They are for the game 'Simon says'.

1   Which instructions are clear?
2   What is missing in the instructions?

1	Simon says, "Move 4 steps forward"
2	Simon says, "Move"
3	Simon says, "Run"
4	Simon says, "Clap your hands two times"
5	Simon says, "Run to the tree"

You will learn:

- that an algorithm is a precise set of instructions
- that programs tell computers what to do
- how to write programs from algorithms.

In this unit, you will learn about algorithms and programs.

Warm up

You will need a sheet of paper. Follow the instructions below.

1   Draw a rectangle.

2   Draw a triangle over the rectangle.

3   In the rectangle, draw three small squares.

   - Show your drawing to your classmates.

   - Do your pictures look different?

The instructions are to draw an object. Your teacher will show you.

Talk in groups. Why are some people's drawings different?

Do you remember?

Before starting this unit, check that you:

- know what an algorithm is
- can follow an algorithm
- know that the order of instructions is important
- know that algorithms are used to write code.

In this unit, you will use ScratchJr. There is an online chapter all about ScratchJr.

Algorithms
Be precise

Learn

An algorithm is a **precise** set of instructions. The instructions need to be in the correct order. An algorithm that is not precise can lead to the wrong result.

In the **Warm up**, you were asked to draw a house.

However, the instructions were not precise.

Here are two algorithms for making a chocolate milkshake.

Algorithm 1

Step	Instruction
1	Pour milk
2	Add chocolate powder
3	Stir

Algorithm 2

Step	Instruction
1	Pour milk in glass
2	Add 1 spoon of chocolate powder
3	Stir for 1 minute

Which algorithm is more precise?

 Hint: Which instructions are clearer?

Keyword
precise: exact, clear and correct

Practise

1   Choose all the words that describe an algorithm.

(exact)   (unclear)   (wrong)   (clear)   (correct)

2   Here are two algorithms to prepare a bowl of cereal with milk. Choose the algorithm that is more precise.

Algorithm 1

Step	Instruction
1	Get cereal
2	Pour cereal
3	Pour milk

Algorithm 2

Step	Instruction
1	Get bowl, cereal and milk
2	Pour cereal in bowl
3	Pour milk in bowl

3   Help Kai get home. Complete this algorithm. Two instructions are missing. Add the most precise instructions.

Step	Instruction
1	Start
2	
3	
4	Stop

(Move up)

(Go to the right 11 steps)

(Walk right)

(Move up 6 steps)

Programs and algorithms
Giving instructions

An algorithm is a precise set of instructions to complete a task.

A **program** is a set of instructions that a computer understands.

An algorithm must be turned into a program for a computer to run it.

A computer carries out a task by following program instructions.

A program is created when each step in an algorithm is changed into **code**.

The algorithm below moves an object 12 steps right.

Algorithm

Step	Instruction	
1	Start on Green Flag	🏳
2	Move right (12)	**12** ➡
3	Stop	STOP

The instructions in a program must be precise.
This is because computers are machines. They follow instructions.

Start on Green Flag ← [🚩 ▪▪▪➡] → Stop

12

Move right 12 steps

We can use the algorithm to create a program in ScratchJr.

Did you know?

Computer games are examples of programs!

Keywords

program: a set of instructions for a computer

code: the instructions in a program

13

Practise

1   Say if the sentences are true or false.

Sentences		True/False
a	Computers can think on their own.	
b	Instructions for a computer must be unclear.	
c	Computer games are examples of programs.	
d	A computer follows a program to do a task.	

2   Which ONE of the two options can a computer carry out?

A

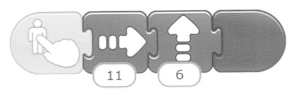

B

Step	Instruction
1	Start on Tap
2	Move right (11)
3	Move up (6)
4	Stop program

3   Look at the algorithm and code below.

Algorithm

Step	Instruction
1	Start on Green Flag
2	Move right (11)
3	Jump (2)
4	Stop program

Code

a   Does the code match the algorithm?

b   Give a reason for your answer.

Coding
Algorithms to programs

Learn

To produce a program, we must write an algorithm.
Each step in the algorithm is changed to code.
Let us look at this task.
We want the **Whale** to spin around. We want it to do a full right spin.
There are FOUR steps to create the program.

Step 1: Break the task into smaller tasks.
- Add a Background.
- Add one character: the **Whale**.
- Add one main action – the **Whale** spins around.

Look at the algorithm for the **Whale** in Step 2.

It is good to write an algorithm before writing code.

15

Step 2: Write an algorithm for the task

This is an algorithm for the **Whale** to do a full right spin.
The **Whale** spins when tapped.

Step	Instruction	
①	Start on Tap	👆
②	Spin right (12)	**12** ↻
③	Stop program	STOP

Step 3: Match a block of code to each instruction in the algorithm

Here is the program for the **Whale** to make a full spin.

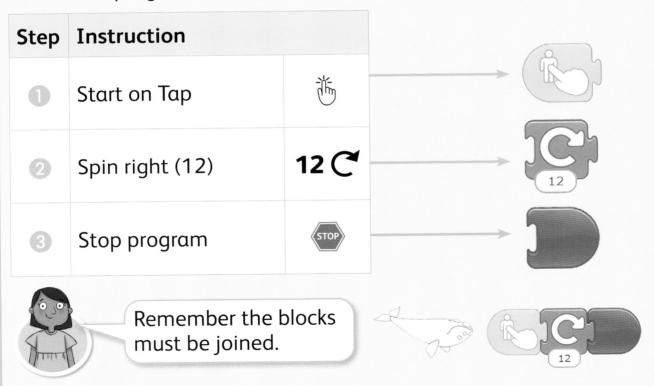

Step	Instruction	
①	Start on Tap	👆
②	Spin right (12)	**12** ↻
③	Stop program	STOP

Remember the blocks must be joined.

Step 4: Run the program

Tap on the **Whale** to see if it does a full right spin.

Practise

We will create a program for the **Whale** to do a full left spin.

1   Look at the algorithm for the **Whale** character.

Whale algorithm

Step	Instruction	
❶	Start on Green Flag	🚩
❷	Spin left (12)	**12** ↺
❸	Stop program	STOP

a   Open ScratchJr.

b   Add a Background like this.

c   Add the **Whale** character.

d   Choose the correct blocks of code to match the algorithm.

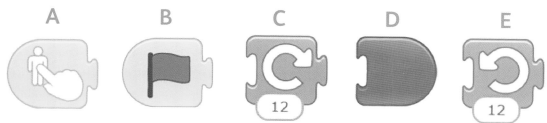

A   B   C   D   E

2   Add the blocks of code for the **Whale** in ScratchJr.

3   Run your code. Does the **Whale** spin left?

Run the program. The **Whale** should do a full left spin.

Go further

1   Here are two algorithms for a **Crab**. The **Crab** should:

   - spin around 2 times
   - say "I am dizzy!"

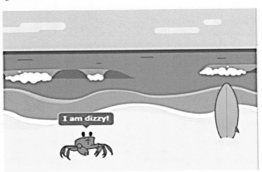

Which algorithm is more precise?

Crab algorithm 1

Step	Instruction
1	Start
2	Spin
3	Talk
4	Stop

Crab algorithm 2

Step	Instruction
1	Start on Tap
2	Spin right (24)
3	Say "I am dizzy!"
4	Stop program

2   Choose the correct blocks of code to match this algorithm. One step is done for you.

Algorithm			Program
Step	**Instruction**		**Block of Code**
❶	Start on Tap	👆	
❷	Spin right (24)	**24 ↻**	
❸	Say "I am dizzy!"	💬	
❹	Stop program	STOP	A

A   B   C   D   E

3   Create the program in ScratchJr.

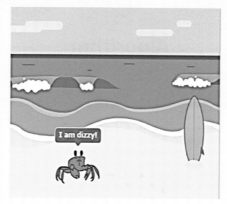

a   Open ScratchJr.

b   Add a Background as shown.

c   Add the **Crab** character.

d   Add the blocks of code you chose in question **2**.

e   Run the program.

Challenge yourself!

Algorithmic thinking

1   Clara follows this path to her house.

Complete the algorithm for Clara. Choose the correct numbers to fill in the blanks for Steps 4 and 5.

Algorithm

Step	Instruction	
①	Start on Green Flag	⚑
②	Move up (3)	3 ↑
③	Move right (1)	1 →
④	Move up ___	? ↑
⑤	Move right ___	? →
⑥	Stop	STOP

2 Here is an algorithm for a girl to:
   • jump
   • do a full spin and
   • say "I did it!"

Step	Instruction	Block of code
❶	Start on Green Flag	
❷	Jump (3)	
❸	Spin right (12)	
❹	Say "I did it!"	
❺	Stop program	

Choose the correct blocks of code to match the algorithm.

A   B   C   D   E   F   G

3 Create a program in ScratchJr.
   a Open ScratchJr.
   b Add a Background as shown.
   c Add a **Child** character.
   d Add the blocks of code you chose in question **2**.
   e Run the program.

My project

1   Work in groups.

Which algorithm is more precise, Algorithm 1 or Algorithm 2?

Algorithm 1

Step	Instruction
❶	Start on Tap
❷	Move up 5 steps
❸	Spin right (12)
❹	Spin left (12)
❺	Move right (10)
❻	Stop program

Algorithm 2

Step	Instruction
❶	Start
❷	Move up
❸	Turn
❹	Turn
❺	Move right
❻	Stop program

2   Which program matches Algorithm 1?

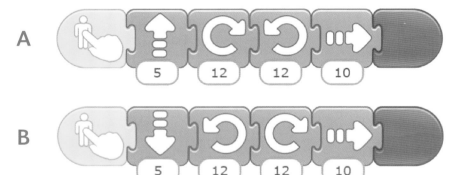

3   Create a program in ScratchJr.
    a   Open ScratchJr.
    b   Add a Background like this.
    c   Add the **Pilot** character.
    d   Add the blocks of code you chose in question **2**.
    e   Run the code.

4 Open the program that was created in question **3**. Add a **Chicken** character like this.

The **Chicken** must do the following when tapped.

- Say "Help!"
- Move right (13)
- Jump (2)
- Stop

a Use the algorithm to select and join the correct blocks for the program.

b Run the program.

Did you know?

Scratch and ScratchJr are named after a way of making music called 'scratching'.

What can you do?

Read and review what you can do.

✔ I know an algorithm is a precise set of instructions.

✔ I know that programs tell computers what to do.

✔ I can write a program in ScratchJr.

Awesome job! Now you know more about algorithms and programs.

Categorical data

Get started!

We can show data in pictures.

Favourite colour	Number of students
Red	
Blue	
Green	
Yellow	
Pink	

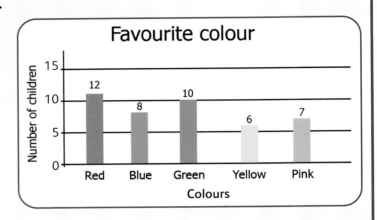

Work with a partner.

1 Point to the bar graph.

2 Point to the pictogram.

3 What do the charts show?

Hint: Which graph has bars? Which chart has pictures?

You will learn:

• about storing data and information on computers

• how to use a computing device to present data

• about collecting data for a reason.

In this unit, you will learn about grouping data.

Warm up

1   Work in pairs. Put the animals in the correct boxes.
    An animal can be in more than one box.

Water animals

Land animals

Animals that fly

2   Can you think of any other ways to group the animals?

Do you remember?

Before starting this unit, check that you:
- know that computing devices can answer questions
- know that computing devices can sort and organise data
- know that computing devices can record data
- know about data tables.

Computer data storage
Advantages

Learn

Computers can store data and information. This is a good idea because:

1	Computers can store lots of data.	
2	Searching for data is quick and easy.	
3	The data can be presented in different ways such as graphs and charts.	
4	Data can be shared across computers.	
5	Data can be added or changed using a computer.	
6	It is easy to copy data. This means data can be replaced if it is lost. A copy of data is called a backup.	

Keyword
backup: a copy of data that is stored in a safe place

Practise

1   Say if the statements are true or false.

Statement		True or false?
a	Making changes to data on a computer is hard. 	
b	Data can be shared across computers.	
c	It is hard to copy data on computers.	

2   Circle the picture that shows a faster way to find a book at the library.

A

B

3   Circle the picture that shows the best way to store lots of data.

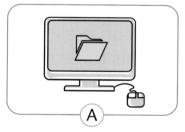
A

B

4   Circle the picture that shows the easier way to get graphs and charts.

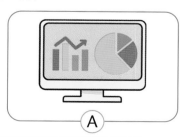
A

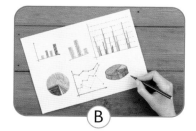
B

Data
Presenting data in groups

Learn

Some data can be put into groups.

For example, data about eye colour can be put into four groups: amber, green, blue, brown.

Software is used to **present** data in different ways.

Data can be shown as a bar graph or pictogram.

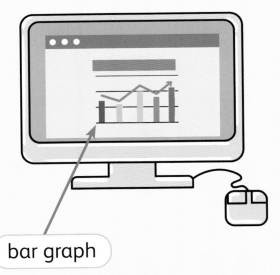

bar graph

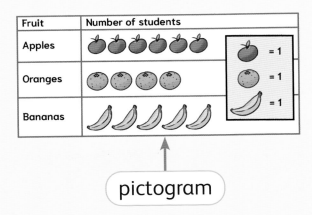

Fruit	Number of students	
Apples	🍎🍎🍎🍎🍎🍎	🍎 = 1
Oranges	🍊🍊🍊🍊	🍊 = 1
Bananas	🍌🍌🍌🍌🍌	🍌 = 1

pictogram

We can present the data in this table as a bar graph or a pictogram.

Name	Favourite colour
Zara	red
Viti	red
David	blue
Jack	green
Annay	green
Sara	green
Liam	green

Keyword
present: to show

Step 1: Count the number of people that like each colour. Draw a data table like this one.

Favourite colour	Number of people
red	2
blue	1
green	4

Step 2: Use an online chart creator. Your teacher will help you.

Once you are on the website, choose the **Bar** option at the top.

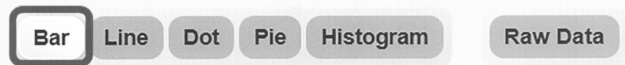

Type the text below. (The data and labels are from the table in Step 1.)

X: Colours   **Y**: Number of people

Title: Favourite colours

Values: 2, 1, 4

Labels: red, blue, green

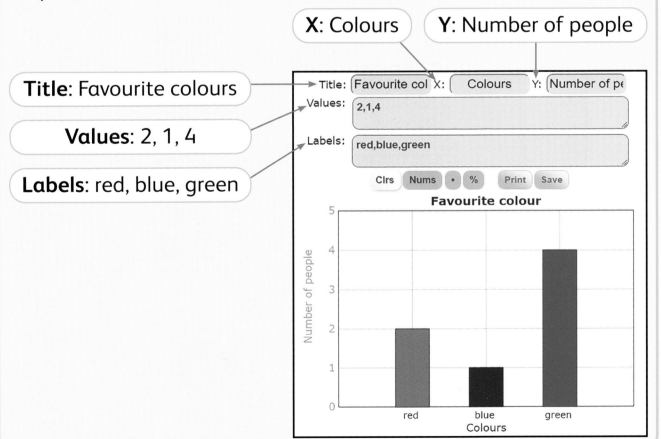

To change the colour of the bars/columns:
- Click on the column/bar.
- Click on the drop-down arrow.
- Choose the colour you want.

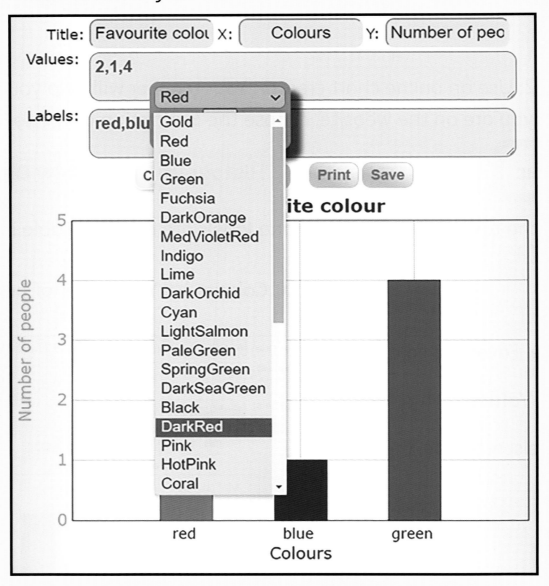

Title: Favourite colou X: Colours Y: Number of peo

Values: 2,1,4

Red ⌄
Gold
Red
Blue
Green
Fuchsia
DarkOrange
MedVioletRed
Indigo
Lime
DarkOrchid
Cyan
LightSalmon
PaleGreen
SpringGreen
DarkSeaGreen
Black
DarkRed
Pink
HotPink
Coral

Labels: red,blu

Print Save

ite colour

Number of people

red   blue   green
Colours

> Wow, you created your first chart!

Practise

For these questions, use the website your teacher gives you.

1   Use data from the table to make a bar graph.

Name	Favourite fruit
Zara	Banana
Viti	Banana
David	Orange
Jack	Orange
Annay	Orange
Sara	Banana
Liam	Apple

Hint: First, count the data. Put it in a table or tally chart, like this:

Favourite fruit	Number of people
Banana	3
Orange	
Apple	

Computing devices
Collecting categorical data

Learn

We can collect data and put it into groups or **categories**. Computing devices collect categorical data every day for different reasons. Data can be collected in different ways. Let us look at some of the ways to collect and use data.

Electronic forms

One way to collect data is by using an electronic form. People can complete electronic forms on devices such as laptops, desktops, smartphones and tablets. For example, schools may collect data on students' activities and likes. They can ask students to complete and submit a form. The answer to each question can be put into different categories.

Question 1 has two categories: Yes, No.

1 Are you a member of any clubs outside of school?

Yes or No

○ Yes

○ No

Question 2 has five categories: Chess, Robotics, Book, Math, Other.

2 Indicate the clubs that you are interested in

Checkbox

☐ Chess

☐ Robotics

☐ Book

☐ Math

☐ Other:

Question 3 has three categories: 1, 2, 3 – where 1 is the lowest rating and 3 is the highest rating.

3 Indicate how much you like this club

Rating Scale

1   2   3

I don't really like it   ○   ○   ○   I love it

Three types of questions that can be included on a form to collect categorical data are: Yes/No, Checkboxes and Rating Scale.

Traffic systems

Traffic systems count the traffic on roads.

They can group different types of traffic, such as:

cars

bicycles

lorries

pedestrians

Once collected, the results can be shown as graphs or charts.

Supermarkets

At a supermarket, each item has a **barcode**. The barcode contains data about the item such as what type of food it is and its price.

At the check-out, a computerised till can read the barcode. It collects data about how many items were sold each day. Items can then be grouped into categories, such as:

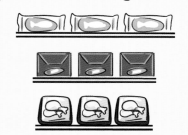

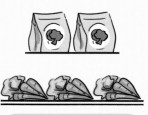

dairy

meat

vegetables

This data shows how much meat was sold on one day, or which vegetable was the most popular in June.

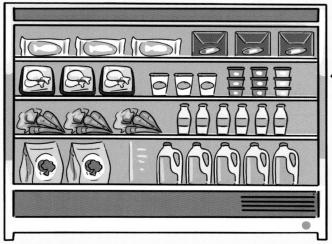

Did you know?

Online shopping sites use data to help you find what you are looking for.

Practise

1 Circle the computing devices that can be used to complete an electronic form.

2 Draw a line to match the questions to the question types.

A Yes/No	Indicate the clubs that you are interested in ☐ Chess ☐ Robotics ☐ Book
B Rating scale	Are you a member of any clubs outside of school? ○ Yes ○ No
C Checkbox	Indicate how much you like this club 1 2 3 I don't really like it ○ ○ ○ I love it

3 Tick (✔) the device a supermarket uses to collect data.

A Camera   ☐

B Barcode reader   ☐

C Monitor   ☐

Go further

1   Say if these statement are true or false.

   a   A computer can only present data in bar graphs.

   b   Lost data can be replaced with backup copies.

   c   It is very difficult to share data and information on a computer.

   d   It is hard to search for data on a computer.

2   Match the descriptions on the left with the computing devices or technologies on the right.

A Can group different types of vehicles	Computerised till
B Can collect data on students' likes	Traffic system
C Scans barcodes on items	Electronic form

Challenge yourself!

1   Fill in the correct answers. Choose from the words in the word bank.

(pictogram)   (bar graph)   (backup)

a   A copy of data is a called a _____.

b   Data can be presented as a _____.

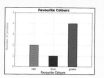

c   Data can be presented as a _____.

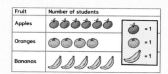

2   Give TWO advantages of storing data on a computer.

3   Use the data table to produce a bar graph. Follow the steps from the **Learn** panel – Presenting categorical data. Use this website to create the charts:

www.mathsisfun.com/data/data-graph.php

Favourite candy	Number of people
Chocolate	9
Gummies	7
Lollipops	5
Toffees	2

My project

1 Work in groups.

a Ask seven students what their favourite candy is. They must choose from the four candies in the table.

b Complete the table with the data you collect.

Favourite candy	Number of people
Chocolate	
Gummies	
Lollipops	
Toffees	

c Follow the steps in the **Learn** panel on pages 29–30. Create a chart from the data you collect. Use this website to create the chart:

www.mathsisfun.com/data/data-graph.php

2 Jasmine wants to know the eye colours in her class.

a What can she use to collect data from her classmates?

b State TWO computing devices that her classmates can use to enter the data.

c What type of question is best for collecting data on eye colour?

A Yes/No

B Checkbox

C Rating scale

What can you do?

Read and review what you can do.

✔ I know why data and information are stored on computers.

✔ I know how to use a computing device to present data.

✔ I know that computing devices collect data for a reason.

> Awesome job! You now know about storing data and how computing devices collect and present data!

Unit 3 Computers and their functions

Computers consist of hardware and software

Discuss with your partner:

What do you use computers for?

Playing games

Watching movies

Sending messages

Video calling friends

Listening to music

You will learn:

- about hardware and software
- that some features make digital devices easy to use
- about the difference between input and output devices.

In this unit, you will learn about hardware and software.

Warm up

Work in pairs.

- Point to pictures of computing devices.
- Point to pictures of software.

Do you remember?

Before starting this unit, check that you:
- know that computers can do different things
- know that computers can run many different programs.

Functions of hardware and software

Computer devices look different. However, they are all made from hardware and software.

Hardware

Hardware are the physical objects that make up a computing device. Here are some examples of hardware:

This processor is hardware. It is hidden inside all computing devices. You cannot see it, but a computing device cannot work without it.

Mia uses a keyboard to write a letter to her friend on the computer. The keyboard is hardware.

Zhu can use headphones to listen to music on her smartphone. Headphones are hardware.

A hard drive stores data and information for later use. Most hard drives are hidden in computers.

Hard drives are hardware.

Keywords

hardware: physical objects that make up a computer

software: a set of instructions for a computer

app: a program that performs a task

Software

Software is another name for a computer program. Software is a set of instructions. Software tells hardware what to do. Without software, hardware cannot do anything.

- Some software controls the computing device.
- Other software does a task. This kind of software is called an **app**.

Here are some examples of software:

File software lets users open, close, save and delete files.

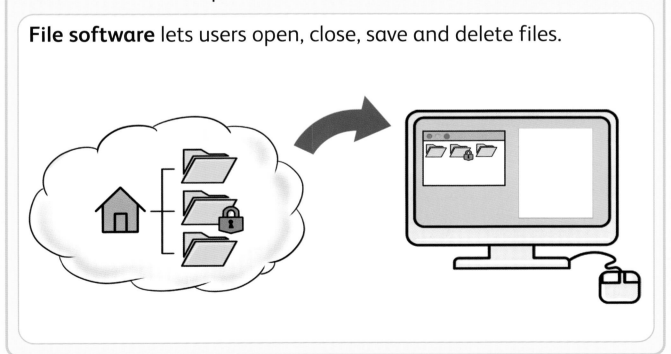

Software that controls the computer lets users enter a password. For example, Mithali enters a password on her computer at school.

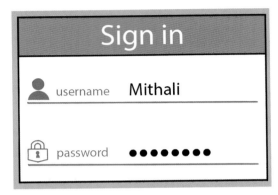

Apps can be used to:

- **create documents**
- **search** for information
- **create** pictures
- **play games**.

This is just a short list.
Apps can be created to do almost anything!

Practise

Say if the following statements are true or false.

Statement	True or false?
a Software lets you play games. **Game***Play*	
b A monitor is software.	
c A processor is software hidden inside a computer.	
d Software can be used to create pictures.	
e Hardware lets you hear sounds made by a computer.	

Hardware and software work together for the computer to function.

Features of digital devices

Learn

Some examples of digital devices include:
- tablets
- smartphones
- desktops
- laptop computers.

There are features of digital devices that make them easy to use. A device that is easy to use is known as a **user-friendly** device.

When we can easily carry a device, we say it is **portable**. How portable a device is depends on its size and weight.

Wireless devices are not connected to a computer with a wire. This makes them easier to use.

There are wireless keyboards, a wireless mouse, and wireless headphones.

Some devices have a large screen. This makes it easier to see information.

Touchscreens let you enter data and information by touching the screen.

Touchscreens also let you zoom in on a part of the screen.

The functions of a device can also make it easy to use.

For instance, a smartphone can show users where they are on a map. This makes it easier to use than a paper map.

Keywords
user-friendly: how easy something is to use
function: the things that a device can do
portable: easy to carry

Practise

Work in pairs.
Fill in the blanks using the word bank to complete the conversation:

(user-friendly) (portable) (screen) (wireless)

Sanchia: I got a new digital device.

Maris: Is it easy to use? If it is, then we say it is _____.

Sanchia: I don't know.

Maris: Does it have a large _____?

Sanchia: Yes it does. It makes the information easier to see!

Maris: Can you easily carry it with you?

Sanchia: Yes. It is _____.

Maris: Do you need wires to connect to it?

Sanchia: No, it is _____.

Maris: I think your new device is easy to use!

Did you know?

You can connect a smartphone to a smart television. This lets you see information on a larger screen.

Differences between input and output devices

Learn

An **input device** is hardware that is used to enter data and information.

Examples of input devices include:

mouse   keyboard   microphone

webcam   games controller   scanner

An **output device** is also hardware. However, it is used so that data or information can be seen or heard.

Examples of output devices include:

headphones   speakers   printer   monitor/screen

Keywords

input device: hardware that puts data into a digital device

output device: hardware that lets us hear or see information

Practise

Complete the sentences using words from the word bank.

Word bank			
mouse	video camcorder	speakers	keyboard
printer	games controller	microphone	headphones

1 Gia is recording the school play with her

_____ _____.

2 She uses a _____ _____ to play games with her brother.

3 She types with a _____.

4 She prints the letter using a _____.

5 Jason likes to play music on his laptop. He uses his

_____ to hear the music.

6 However, he can use his _____ if he does not

want to disturb anyone.

Go further

Work in pairs.

1 Look at the pictures below. Match them to the names in the word bank.

2 Point to the input devices in the word bank.

3 Point to the output devices in the word bank.

4 Point to the storage devices in the word bank.

> **Word bank**
>
> keyboard, mouse, microphone, camera, printer, monitor, speakers, headphones, hard drive, flash/USB drive

Challenge yourself!

Work in groups.

1   Circle the portable computer devices in the picture.

2   What makes a tablet easy to use?

3   Work in groups of four. For each of the following scenarios, say what hardware is being used:

   a   June looks at some photos on her computer.
   b   Mark uses an app to play music on his smartphone.
   c   Camille types a poem on her tablet.
   d   John plays a computer game on his laptop.

My project

1   Work in groups of three. Choose two devices from the list below:
   • desktop computer
   • laptop
   • tablet
   • smartphone.
   Explain what features make each device user-friendly.

2 Tick (✔) the correct column.

Statement	Hardware	Software
a It is another name for a program.		
b It is used to give instructions to hardware.		
c It is used to store data.		
d It is used to search the internet.		
e It is hidden inside all computers.		
f It is used to manage files.		
g It is used to type words into documents.		
h It is used to listen to music.		
i It is used to control the cursor.		

What can you do?

Read and review what you can do.
- ✔ I know the difference between hardware and software.
- ✔ I can say what features make digital devices easy to use.
- ✔ I know the difference between input and output devices.

Great work! Now you know about hardware, software, input and output devices.

Unit 4 Be an animator

Tasks and events

Get started!

Work in groups of three. Tell your friends about:
- the pets you have
- what they eat
- what tasks you do when taking care of pets.

You will learn:
- to find and correct errors in algorithms
- to identify the steps to perform tasks
- to create programs that repeat things.

In this unit, you will create programs that repeat things.

Warm up

Here are the steps for brushing your teeth.

Compare your answer with your partner.

Put them in the correct order.

A Step ___: Brush your teeth left to right.

B Step ___: Put toothpaste on your toothbrush.

C Step ___: Rinse your toothbrush with water.

D Step ___: Rinse your mouth with water.

Do you remember?

Before starting this unit, check that you:
- understand that programs tell computers what to do
- can create programs in ScratchJr.

In this unit, you will use ScratchJr.

There is an online chapter all about ScratchJr.

Algorithms and programs
Errors in algorithms

Learn

We can write algorithms for everyday events and tasks. These can contain errors. An error or mistake is also called a **bug**.

Can you name any everyday events?

Keyword
bug: a mistake in an algorithm or program

Algorithm for rain forming a puddle

Look at the algorithm below. It is for rain forming a puddle.

There is an error in the algorithm.

Step	Instruction
1	Clouds form
2	Water collects in a puddle
3	It starts to rain

The error is that Step 3 should be Step 2.

We can swap Steps 2 and 3.

Now the algorithm is correct.

Step	Instruction
1	Clouds form
2	It starts to rain
3	Water collects in a puddle

Practise

1 We want to walk along the path shown.

The algorithm is written in the table. What is the error?

Step	Instruction	
1	Move right (2)	2 ➡
2	Move down (1)	1 ⬇
3	Move right (5)	5 ➡
4	Move down (1)	1 ⬇

2 In one day, the weather changes in the order below.

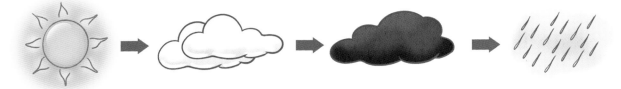

Here is the algorithm for the weather. What is the error?

Step	Instruction
1	Show Sun
2	Show White Clouds
3	Show Rainfall
4	Show Grey Clouds

Steps to complete tasks

To write an algorithm, we need to break down the task into steps.

Look at the example below. It shows the the steps to make a cup of tea.

Algorithm for making a cup of tea

The steps to make a cup of tea are:

Leave for 5 minutes

Remove the teabag

Pour warm water into teacup

Boil water in a kettle

Add milk

Place a teabag in a teacup

Now that we know the steps, we can put them in order.
The steps are in order in this algorithm.

Step	Instruction
1	Boil water in a kettle
2	Place a teabag in a teacup
3	Pour warm water into teacup
4	Leave for 5 minutes
5	Remove the teabag
6	Add milk

When we write an algorithm, we must put the steps in the correct order.

Practise

1 You have been asked to make yellow slime.

   a There are five steps to make yellow slime. One instruction is not needed. Which one? ____

   b Put the instructions in the correct order.

(A)

Measure out the ingredients.

(B)

Mix the ingredients.

(C)

Get the ingredients.

(D)

Make more slime.

(E)

Add yellow colouring.

(F)
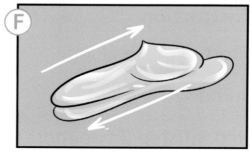
Roll out the slime.

Using repeat

Sometimes, we want to **repeat** some instructions. In ScratchJr, the **Repeat** block is used to repeat instructions.

A repeat command makes writing algorithms and programs easier!

This algorithm and ScratchJr program are for a **Cat**.

Step	Instruction
1	Start on Green Flag
2	Jump (2)
3	Jump (2)
4	Jump (2)
5	Stop program

The **Cat** jumps repeatedly.

We can change the program to use a **Repeat** block. There were three instructions to **Jump (2)**. So, we enter **3** into the **Repeat** block.

Step	Instruction
1	Start on Green Flag
2	Jump (2)
3	Repeat step 2 two more times
4	Stop program

Keyword
repeat: do something again

Practise

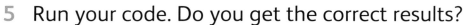

1 Open a new project.

2 Add any Background.

3 Add the **Cat** character.

4 Add the code with the **Repeat** block from page 60.

5 Run your code. Do you get the correct results?

6 Add the **Dog** character.

7 Create a program for the **Dog** that uses the **Repeat** block to match the algorithm below.

Step	Instruction
1	Start on Tap
2	Say "Woof!"
3	Move Right (2)
4	Move Right (2)
5	Move Right (2)
6	Say "Woof!"
7	Stop program

8 Run your completed program.

Explain to your partner what the **Repeat** block does in your program.

Go further

1   Liam is getting dressed for school. What is the error in the algorithm?

> Step ① Put on T-shirt

> Step ② Put on trousers

> Step ③ Put on shoes

> Step ④ Put on socks

Computational thinking

What are some additional steps to get dressed if it is winter time? Write a new algorithm to get dressed during winter.

2   Here is an algorithm for a **Seahorse** character.

Step	Instruction
①	Start on Green Flag
②	Move up 4
③	Move up 4
④	Shrink by 2
⑤	Shrink by 2
⑥	Shrink by 2
⑦	Stop program

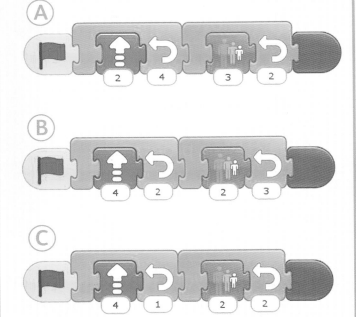

Which program does the same thing as this algorithm?

Challenge yourself!

1   Start a new project. Add the correct code from the **Go further** activity to the **Seahorse** character.

2   Add a **Fish** character.

3   Create a program for the **Fish** to match this algorithm.

Step	Instruction
❶	Start on Green Flag
❷	Say "Hi Seahorse"
❸	Move right (6)
❹	Move left (2)
❺	Play pop sound
❻	Repeat steps 3 to 5 two more times
❼	Stop program

Test your code to see if you get the correct results.

4   Add the **Starfish** character to your project.

5   Add the code below to the **Starfish** and run it.

6   Change the code for the **Starfish** so it uses the **Repeat** block. The new code should get the same results.

7   Run your final program.

My project

1 Look at the algorithm to get out of a maze. It has one error. What is the error? How would you correct it?

Algorithm
Move right (2)
Move up (3)
Move right (4)
Move up (1)

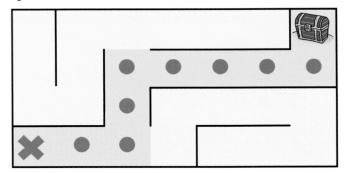

2 Think about the things you do every night when you go to bed. Write an algorithm for going to bed. Include all the things you do in the correct order.

3 a Create a program from the algorithm below for the **Basketball** character. Use the **Repeat** block.

Step	Instruction
1	Start on Green Flag
2	Jump (1)
3	Move right (2)
4	Jump (1)
5	Move right (2)
6	Jump (1)
7	Move right (2)
8	Stop program

Include the start and end steps in your algorithm.

b Run your code and check that you get the correct results.

Did you know?

Google uses algorithms for its search engine. Its newest search algorithm is named **Hummingbird**.

What can you do?

Read and review what you can do.

✔ I can find and correct errors in algorithms.

✔ I can identify the steps to perform tasks.

✔ I can create programs that use the repeat command.

Good job! Now you can create algorithms and programs that repeat instructions.

Network devices

Get started!

Look at the two pictures of remote control toy cars.

Discuss with your partner what the differences are between the two cars.

- Tell your partner which type of car you like best.
- Tell your partner why you like the chosen car.
- How does the controller send messages to the car?

You will learn:

- that different devices can connect to a network
- that two devices can work together
- to explain the terms *wired* and *wireless* networks.

In this unit, you will learn about wired and wireless networks.

Warm up

Discuss these questions with your partner.

1   What is a network?
2   What devices do you know that cannot connect to a network?
3   What is the internet?

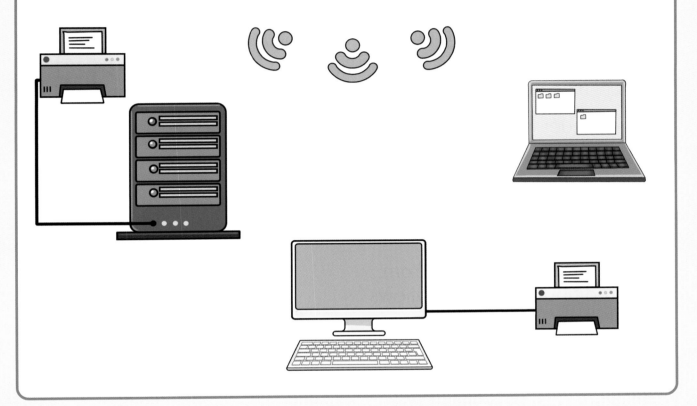

Do you remember?

Before starting this unit, check that you:
- know that devices can connect to make a network
- know that the internet is made of many computers connected together
- know that some devices are connected by wires and other devices are not
- know there are times when the internet is not available.

Networks
Network devices

Keyword
edit: to make changes or corrections

Learn

You already know that desktops, laptops, tablets and smartphones can connect to a network and the internet.

Many other devices can also connect to a network and the internet. Below are some of these devices.

An e-reader is used to read ebooks.

E-readers can connect to the internet without wires.

A scanner takes images from printed photographs. It allows a user to **edit** the images on a computer.

Scanners can connect to a network with or without wires.

A photocopier makes copies of documents.

These copies can be sent to a computer.

A photocopier can connect to a network with or without wires.

A smart TV lets users view movies and shows. It also runs apps.

Smart TVs can connect to a network with or without wires. This allows users to stream movies and play games over the internet.

A smart music system connects speakers in different rooms.

It can be controlled using another device like a smartphone or tablet.

It connects to a network without wires.

A smart bulb is a special light bulb that is connected to the internet.

It can be controlled using an app.

A smart bulb connects to a network without wires.

Smart bulbs can change colour and turn themselves on automatically.

A home security camera records a video of a house. The video can be seen on a smartphone tablet or computer.

These cameras can connect to a network with or without wires.

Practise

1 Point to each device and say its name.

2 Choose the correct answer to complete each sentence.

a A home security camera can connect to a network _____.

| with wires | without wires | with or without wires |

b A scanner can connect to a network _____.

| with wires | without wires | with or without wires |

c A photocopier can connect to a network _____.

| with wires | without wires | with or without wires |

d An e-reader can connect to a network _____.

| with wires | without wires | with or without wires |

e A smart TV can connect to a network _____.

| with wires | without wires | with or without wires |

3 Which of the following devices cannot connect to a network with or without wires?

A 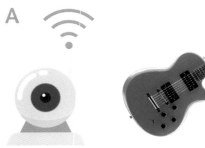 B  C  D

Networks
Devices working together

A device that is not connected to another device is known as a standalone device.

A standalone device cannot talk to other devices.

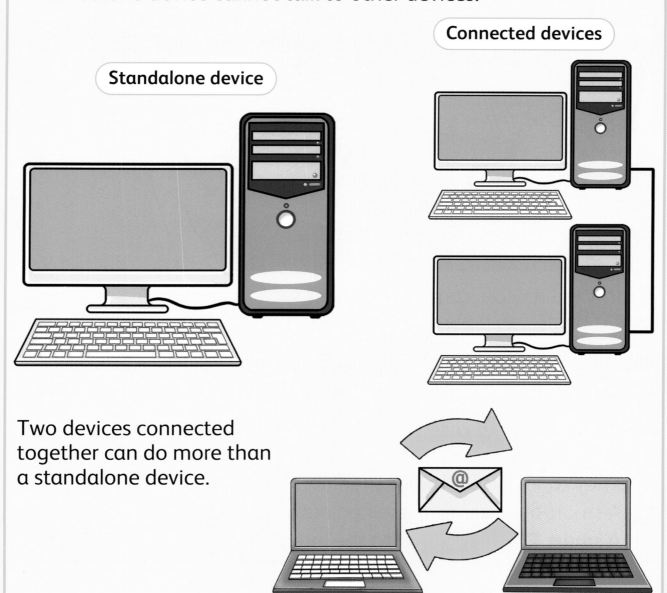

Connected devices

Standalone device

Two devices connected together can do more than a standalone device.

Two connected devices let users send emails or messages.

Connected devices can share devices such as printers. This means that a home can have one printer to share among everyone in the house.

- Connected devices can easily share files such as documents, videos and images.

  A standalone device cannot easily share files.

- 'Smart' household devices can connect to a network.

  They can do more things than normal household appliances.

  A smart bulb can turn itself on automatically.

  A smart TV can connect to the internet.

Practise

1   Say if these statements are true or false.

Statement	True or false?
a Two connected devices can do more than one device.	
b Two connected devices can talk to each other.	
c Users on two connected devices cannot share printers.	
d Files can be shared if two devices are connected together.	
e A standalone device can talk to other devices.	

2   Tick (✔) the standalone device.

A    B

3   Say if you will need a standalone or a connected device to make the following tasks easier.

Task	Standalone or connected device?
a Type a letter on a desktop	
b Send the letter to your friend	
c Print the letter	

Did you know?

The first large computer network was called ARPANET. It was developed in 1969.

Internet
Wired and wireless networks

Learn

There are two types of networks: wireless and wired.

Wireless networks

A network connected without wires is called a wireless network.

Devices connected to wireless networks can move around and stay connected.

Wireless networks are popular in homes and cafes.

Laptops, tablets and smartphones often connect to wireless networks.

Wired networks

A wired network uses cables to connect devices.

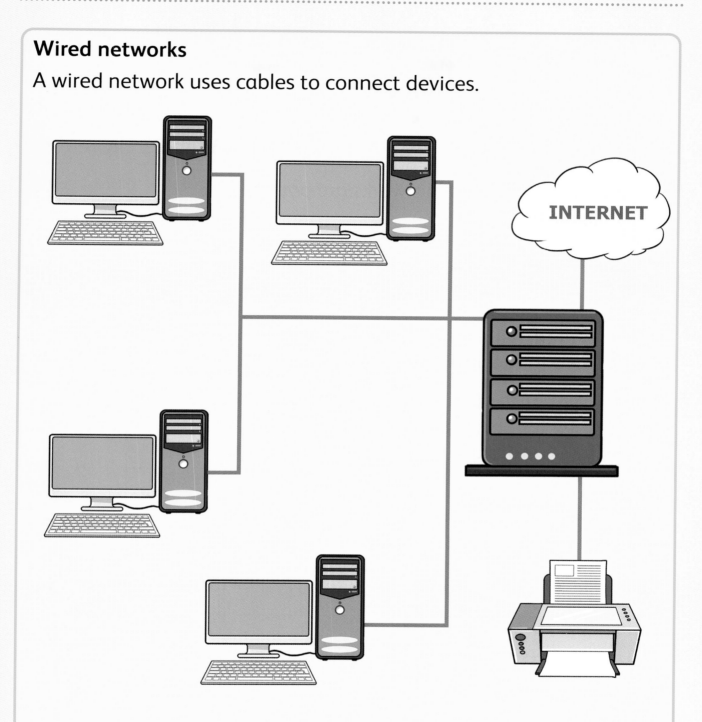

Devices connected to wired networks do not move around.

Wired networks are often used in businesses or schools.

A good example of a device that connects to a wired network is a desktop computer.

Practise

1 Complete the sentences. Choose the correct word in brackets by ticking (✔) the column.

Sentence	Wired	Wireless
a (Wired/Wireless) networks are popular in homes.		
b (Wired/Wireless) networks are popular in offices.		
c (Wired/Wireless) networks are normally used for devices that can move around.		
d (Wired/Wireless) networks are normally used for devices that do not move around.		
e Smartphones normally connect to (wired/wireless) networks.		
f Desktops normally connect to (wired/wireless) networks.		

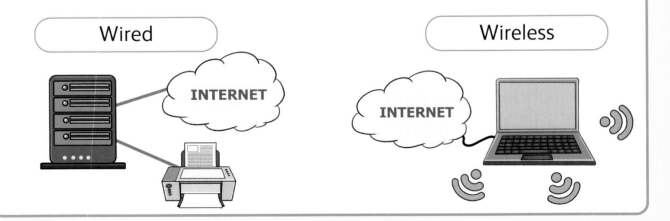

Wired

Wireless

INTERNET

INTERNET

Go further

1   Draw a wired network with three devices. Write the names of the devices.

2   Draw a wireless network with three devices. Write the names of the devices.

3   Complete the table. Cut out each statement and paste it below the correct heading in the table.

Wired network	Wireless network

devices connected without wires   often used in schools

often used in homes   devices connected with wires

users can move around easily with their device

devices do not normally move

Challenge yourself!

1 a Give one example of a place where wireless networks may be used.

b Give one reason why it may be used there.

c Name some devices that can be part of the network.

2 a Give one example of a place where a wired network is used.

b Give one reason why it may be used there.

c Name some devices that can be part of the network.

3 Tell your partner about the differences between a wired and wireless network.

4 Say if these statements are true or false.

Statement	True or false?
a A standalone device can share information on a network.	
b Connected devices can communicate via email.	
c Connected devices cannot share devices like printers.	
d 'Smart' household appliances can connect to a network.	
e Two devices working together can do things one device cannot do on its own.	

My project

The school principal is thinking about building a computer network. The principal has some questions.

Can you help the principal to answer these questions?

1   What are the benefits of connecting two devices together?

2   Which of these devices can connect to a wired network?

   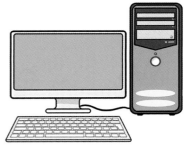

3   Name three devices that commonly connect to a wireless network.

4   List three devices that can connect to both wired AND wireless networks.

5   Draw a sketch of each type of network.

What can you do?

Read and review what you can do.

✔ I know about devices that can connect to a network.

✔ I know that two devices can work together.

✔ I know how to explain the terms *wired* and *wireless* networks.

Good work! Now you know more about wired and wireless networks.

Unit 6 Be a designer

Dance routine

Get started!

Work in groups of four. Discuss what types of dances you like. Take turns to show your group your favourite dance moves.

What are the steps in your dance?

You will learn:

- to follow and understand algorithms
- to plan instructions for characters in programs
- about working with others when debugging programs.

In this unit, you will create algorithms and programs in ScratchJr.

Warm up

Work in pairs. Look at the moves in the dance routine below.

There is a pattern in the moves.

Discuss with your partner what you think is the next move.

Do you remember?

Before starting this unit, check that you:
- understand that algorithms are a set of instructions
- know algorithms can be created as programs
- know that 'debugging' means correcting errors.

In this unit, you will use ScratchJr. There is an online chapter all about ScratchJr.

Writing algorithms and programs
Understanding algorithms

Learn

An algorithm is a set of instructions to complete a task.

These instructions need to be in the correct order.

A dancer moves from point 1 to point 2 as shown below.

Algorithm A and B are instructions for the dancer. However, only one algorithm is correct.

Algorithm A

1   Move 2 blocks down
2   Move 2 blocks down
3   Move 3 blocks right
4   Move 1 block right

Algorithm B

1   Move 2 blocks down
2   Move 3 blocks right
3   Move 2 blocks down
4   Move 1 block right

Read both algorithms. Can you see that Algorithm B is correct?

Algorithm A is not correct. Steps 2 and 3 are in the wrong order. This means the dancer does not reach point 2.

Practise

Look at the path a singer walks while on stage.

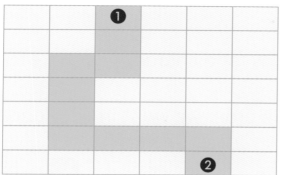

She walks from point 1 to point 2.

1   Put the steps in the correct order that the singer takes.

> **A** Move 3 blocks down

> **B** Move 1 block down

> **C** Move 2 blocks down

> **D** Move 1 block to the left

> **E** Move 3 blocks to the right

Steps	Algorithm
① **2 ↓**	
② **1 ←**	
③ **3 ↓**	
④ **3 →**	
⑤ **1 ↓**	

2   What is the shortest path from point 1 to point 2? Discuss with your partner what the steps are.

Hint: The shortest path has a total of 2 steps and has two possible solutions.

Planning instructions for characters

Learn

Planning a dance routine

We can plan the instructions for a character's dance routine by writing an algorithm.

The steps are written in the order we want in the dance routine.

Step	Instruction
1	Start on Green Flag
2	Turn left (3)
3	Turn right (3)
4	Jump (2)
5	Move right (1)
6	Move left (1)
7	Stop program

We can change this algorithm into a program.

We write code in ScratchJr for each step.

We use the **Hop** block to jump.

This code is added to a **Person** character in ScratchJr.

When we run the code, we get the results we wanted. This means the program followed the dance routine algorithm correctly.

> In ScratchJr, the number 3 is a quarter turn when using the **Turn Left** or **Turn Right** block.

Practise

Create the program on page 84 by following these steps:

1   Open a new project and add any Background.
2   Add the blocks of code to any **Person** character.
3   Run your program and see what results you get.

We want to add a **Child** character. The **Child** should dance when the **Person** bumps into it.

4   Complete the algorithm for the **Child** character. When bumped into, the **Child** should start dancing. The dance should consist of the following:

- Move up 4 grid squares
- Jump 2 grid squares
- Move left 1 grid square
- Turn right for a full turn (12)

5   Create the code for this algorithm in ScratchJr.
6   To test it, place both characters close enough so that the **Person** bumps into the **Child**.

Step	Instruction
❶	Start on Bump
❷	Move _____
❸	_____ 2
❹	Move _____
❺	Turn _____ 12
❻	Stop program

Debugging programs with others

Learn

A bug is a mistake in an algorithm or program. Finding and removing the mistake is called **debugging**.

> **Keyword**
> **debug:** to find and remove errors in a program

It is good to work with others when debugging programs.

Debugging with others:

- is faster
- makes it easier to find all the bugs
- lets us share knowledge and learn from others.

> Two heads are better than one when debugging programs!

Look at the algorithm and the first program below. The code has one mistake.

Step	Instruction
1	Start on Green Flag
2	Move Right (4)
3	Turn Left (3)
4	Move Up (2)
5	End program

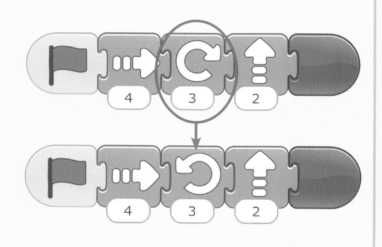

First, we need to find the mistake. Then, we can correct it. We need to change the **Turn Right** block to the **Turn Left** block to correct the program.

Practise

Debugging a program in groups

1   Open a new project.
2   Add a Background of your choice.
3   Add the **Astronaut**. The **Astronaut** should follow these instructions:

Step	Instruction
1	Start on Green Flag
2	Move left (5)
3	Turn right (3)
4	Jump (3)
5	Turn left (3)
6	Move right (5)
7	Stop program

4   Add and run the code above.
5   In groups of three, debug the code.

Were you able to debug the code faster in groups than by yourself?

Go further

1   Look at the path a mouse takes to the cheese. How many blocks must the mouse move to get to the cheese?

Computational thinking

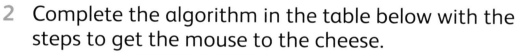

2   Complete the algorithm in the table below with the steps to get the mouse to the cheese.

Step	Instruction
1	Move right _____
2	Move _____
3	Move _____
4	Move _____ (2)

3   The code for the algorithm is on the right. It contains errors. Work in groups of three to find the errors.

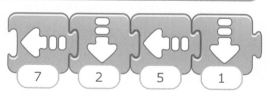

Discuss in your group how you would fix these errors.

Challenge yourself!

1   Open a new project and add a background.
2   Recreate the algorithm in **Go further**. Add it to the **Dog**.
3   Table 1 shows new instructions we want to give to the **Dog**. Change your program to match Table 1.

Table 1	
1	Start on Green Flag
2	Move right (4)
3	Jump (2)
4	Stop program

4   Add the **Butterfly**.
5   Table 2 shows the instructions for the **Butterfly**. Create a program to match Table 2.

Table 2	
1	Start on Tap
2	Move down (2)
3	Grow (2)
4	Repeat step 3 four more times
5	Stop program

6   Run your program. Check that you get the desired results. Work in pairs to debug your programs.

My project

Design a dance routine with your partner.

1 Open a new project in ScratchJr and add any Background.

2 Add a **Child** character and the code below.

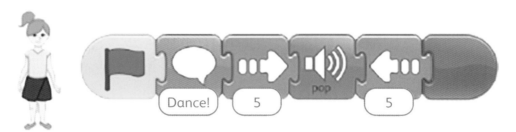

3 Draw a line to match each code block to an instruction.

Code		Instruction
a		Move left (5)
b	Dance!	Stop Program
c	5	Say "Dance!"
d	pop	Start on Green Flag
e	5	Move right (5)
f		Play pop sound

4 Add a **Person** character to your project.

5   Look at the algorithm and code for the **Person**. The program has errors. Find the errors with your partner.

Step	Instruction
❶	Start on Bump
❷	Turn left (1)
❸	Turn right (1)
❹	End program

6   Fix the errors and add the correct code to the **Person**.

7   Test your program. Check that you get the correct results.

Did you know?

The **Mars Climate Orbiter** was a spaceship.

A bug in the program controlling the spaceship caused an error. The mission could not be completed!

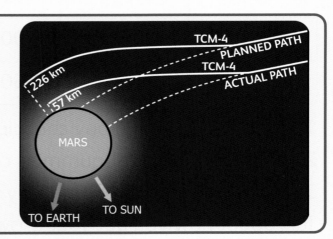

What can you do?

Read and review what you can do.

✔ I can follow and understand algorithms.

✔ I can plan instructions for characters in programs.

✔ I know about the benefits of working with others when debugging programs.

Great! Now you can plan algorithms and work with others to debug programs.

Solving problems

Get started!

Sharlene and her friends are at the candy shop.

Sharlene has $5.00, Joe has $2.00 and Sandy has $2.00.

In pairs, use the data in the table to answer the following questions.

Candy	Quantity	Cost
Chocolate	1 bar	$5.00
Gummies	1 bag	$1.00
Candy corn	1 bag	$1.50

1 Who can afford to buy chocolate?

2 How many bags of gummies can Joe buy?

3 Which candies can Sandy buy?

Talk about how you got your answer.

You will learn:

• about the types of data that a question may generate

• about data that can be recorded using computing devices

• how data may help to solve problems.

In this unit, you will learn about different kinds of data and how they can be used.

Warm up

Draw a line to match each question with the number of answers to be given.

Question	Number of answers
a Ten children are asked their favourite colours.	1 answer
b Susan is asked, "When is your birthday?"	10 answers
c Anna is asked, "What is your form teacher's name?"	20 answers
d Twenty people are asked, "What is your favourite movie?"	1 answer

Do you remember?

Before starting this unit, check that you:
- know about questions that can be answered using a data table
- know how to use computing devices to present data
- know that computing devices collect data for a particular purpose.

Data
Statistical vs non-statistical

Learn

There are different types of questions.

A **statistical question** has more than one answer.

A **non-statistical question** has only one possible answer.

Let us look at some examples of statistical and non-statistical questions.

What are the favourite snacks of the students in Mrs Ali's class?

This is a statistical question. There is more than one possible answer.

How tall are the boys on the basketball team?

This is a statistical question. There is more than one possible answer.

What colour are these words written in?

This is a non-statistical question. There is only one possible answer to this question.

How long is your school day?

This is a non-statistical question. There is only one possible answer to this question.

Practise

1 Say if the following sentences are true or false.

Sentence	True or false?
a A non-statistical question has more than one answer.	
b There are different types of questions.	
c A statistical question has only one possible answer.	

2 Work with a partner. Draw lines to show if each question is statistical or non-statistical. The first one is done for you.

a	How tall are the students in a class?
b	What colour is David's shirt?
c	How many dolls do five children own?
d	What is Janice's shoe size?
e	What are the test scores of 15 students?
f	What is Sheldon's favourite subject?

Statistical

Non-statistical

Computing devices
Statistical data

Learn

You collect statistical data when you ask a statistical question.
Statistical data can be grouped into two categories:
numerical or **categorical**.

Numerical data

Numerical data can be counted or measured.
Here are two examples of numerical data:

The picture shows a teacher collecting the test results from six students.

The reading on the thermometer is 98.6 degrees.

Categorical data

Categorical data can be grouped into categories.
Here are two examples of categorical data:
* eye colour (brown, blue, black, green, amber)
* hair colour (black, brown, blonde).

Categorical data can be given numerical values. For example, you could use:

- the number 1 for black hair
- the number 2 for brown hair
- the number 3 for blonde hair.

However, these numbers do not have any meaning. For example, you could not add them together.

Never try to add, subtract or multiply categorical data!

Computing devices can be used to record data on electronic forms.

These forms can contain categorical and numerical data.

Numerical data is entered by typing or selecting a number.

Categorical data is entered by selecting a category.

1. Do you own any pets?
   Yes ○ No ○
2. How many pets do you own?
   _____
3. Would you like to own another pet?
   1 ○   2 ○   3 ○
   NO   Maybe   Yes, I would love to

Practise

1   Copy the sentences.
    Fill in the blanks with
    the correct words:
    categorical, **statistical**,
    numerical.

Hint: A word can
be used more than
once or not at all.

 a   Two main types of statistical data are _____ and
     _____ data.

 b   _____ data is data that can be counted or
     obtained by measurements.

 c   _____ data are grouped based on characteristics.

2   State if the following data to be collected is **numerical** or
    categorical data. Tick (✔) the correct column.

Data		Numerical	Categorical
a	A teacher collects data on her students' favourite food.		
b	Jodie measures the height of a plant each day. Her measurements are: 5 cm, 7 cm, 6 cm.		
c	Students belong to one of four houses: yellow, blue, red and green.		

3   Draw a line to match the data to the labels.
    a   Rainfall in 3 days: 2 mm, 1 mm, 3 mm
    b   Feelings of students: happy, sad
    c   Number of students in classes: 25, 30, 15
    d   Favourite snack: chips, chocolate, popcorn

Categorical data

Numerical data

Data
Solving problems

Learn

Data is used to help solve problems. We can use data to decide what to do.

Data is used to solve problems in the following ways:

- Teachers record their students' scores. They use this data to see where each student needs help.
- Supermarkets collect data about how many items they sell each day. They use this data to find out how many items are left.

Item name	Original number of items	Number of items sold	Number of items left
Rice	35	20	15
Red beans	20	18	2
Soda	22	12	10

The table shows there are only 2 cans of red beans left.

- Weather forecasts use data about rain and wind. Powerful computers use this data to predict tomorrow's weather.
- Map systems in cars collect data about traffic.

  They use this to calculate the quickest route between one place and another.

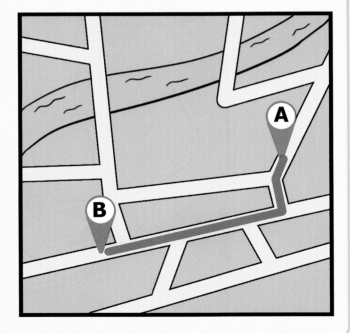

Practise

1 Say if these sentences are true or false.

Sentence	True or false?
a Data is used to solve problems.	
b Data cannot be used to make decisions.	
c Data can be used to predict the future.	

2 Choose the correct options to solve the following problems.

a Mr Clifford wants to know who got the highest mark in class. He needs to …

Option 1	Option 2
Sort the marks in order	Add all the students' marks

b Mrs Fields wants to know which brand of ice cream is cheaper. She needs to …

Option 1	Option 2
Compare the size of the two brands	Compare the price of the two brands

c A teacher needs to know the total number of students going to the museum. He needs to …

Option 1	Option 2
Sort the list of students	Add the number of students

Go further

1 Say if the following data is numerical or categorical.
Tick (✔) the correct column.

Data	Numerical	Categorical
a Jimmy and Caleb have red, green and blue cars.		
b Jimmy has 10 cars and Caleb has 7 cars.		

2 Say if these questions are statistical or non-statistical.

Question	Statistical	Non-statistical
a What are the video game scores of five friends?		
b What school club is Sarah in?		
c Where does your teacher live?		
d What do students in your class have for lunch?		
e How many children are wearing blue and red sweaters today?		

3 Draw lines to match the problem with the data that is needed to solve the problem.

Problem
Number of items in a supermarket
Predicting floods
Helping students to learn

Data
Amount of rainfall
Students' scores
Daily sales of items

Challenge yourself!

1   Mrs Chen sends a questionnaire to 25 students.
The questionnaire has FOUR questions.

① How many siblings do you have?

Your answer _____

② What is your height?

Your answer _____

③ How do you get to school?
- ○   bus
- ○   private car
- ○   ride
- ○   Other _____

④ Do you like school?

No   1   2   3   I love school
           ○   ○   ○

   a   Which two questions collect numerical data?
   b   What device can record the numerical data on the form?
   c   Which two questions collect categorical data?
   d   What device can record categorical data on the form?

2   Which questions could Mrs Chen answer after sending the form?
   A   How tall are the students?
   B   How many students like running?
   C   How do students get to school?

3   Mrs Chen needs to know how many students travel by bus.
   a   What question on the form will give her the data?
   b   What does she need to do with this data?

My project

1   Work in groups. Collect the following data from the members of your group. Include the answers in a table like the one below.

Name	Height	Eye colour

2   State whether each of the following data is numerical or categorical.

   a   Height _____

   b   Eye colour _____

3   Say whether these questions are statistical or non-statistical. Tick (✔) the correct column.

Question	Statistical	Non-statistical
a What is your eye colour?		
b How many students in your class?		
c What are the eye colours in your group?		
d How tall are the students in your group?		

4 a The teacher wants to know how many students have brown eyes. What data is needed? Tick (✔) the correct box(es).

- Eye colour of students ☐

- Name of students ☐

- Height of students ☐

b Who is the tallest student in your group? _____

Did you know?

Data scientists use data to solve a wide range of very complex problems!

What can you do?

Read and review what you can do.

Congratulations! Now you know about solving data problems.

✔ I can talk about types of data that a question may generate.

✔ I know about types of data that can be recorded using computing devices.

✔ I know how data may help to solve problems.

Creating words

Get started!

In groups of three, take turns to:
- Sing the alphabet song.
- Write your first name on a sheet of paper.

You will learn:
- to write instructions to complete tasks
- to program a physical device.

In this unit, you will give directions to a physical device.

Warm up

Work in pairs.

The animals shown below are missing the first letter of their name.

Give your partner instructions to draw the missing letters.

For example, for the Crab the instruction to write 'C' could be:

Draw a line from right to left.

Leave the pencil on the paper and draw another line up.

Leave the pencil on the paper and draw another line from left to right.

Take turns with your partner.

Crab   _urtle   _wl

_nake   _arrot

Do you remember?

Before starting this unit, check that you:
- can give instructions for a task
- can give directions (forward, backward, left, right)
- can run a program
- know that programs can have errors.

Drawing letters

Learn

Algorithm to draw the letter L
Look at the steps to draw the letter 'L'.

Step ①

Start program

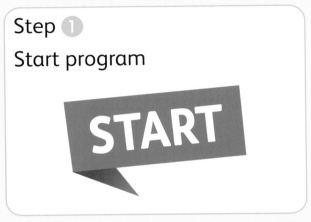

Step ②

Set marker down

Step ③

Turn left

Step ④

Move forward 8 cm

8 cm

Step ⑤

Turn right

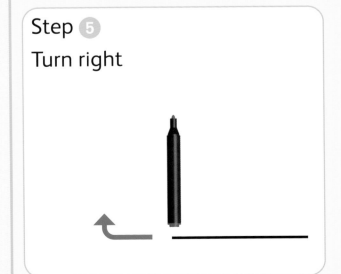

Step ⑥

Move forward 16 cm

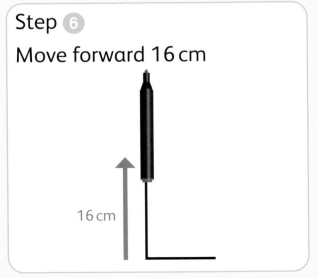

16 cm

Practise

Create the algorithm to draw the letter 'T'.
Put the steps in the correct order. Step 1 is done for you.

Step ___: Move forward 8 cm

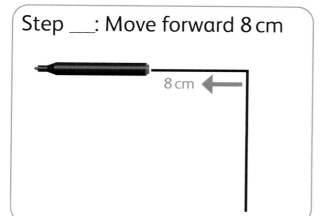

Step 1: Start program

Step ___: Turn left

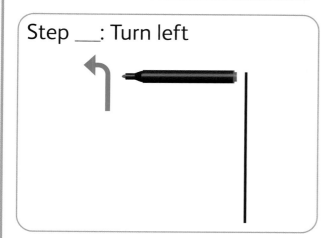

Step ___: Move backward 16 cm

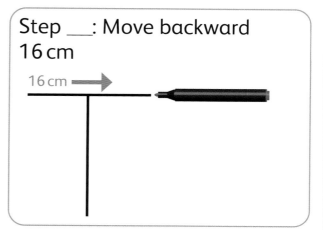

Step ___: Set marker down

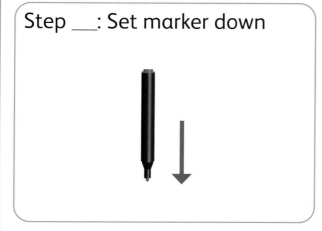

Step ___: Move forward 16 cm

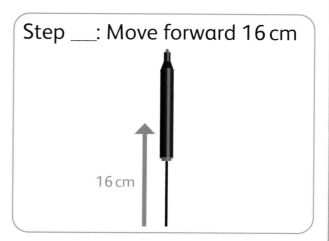

Giving directions
Physical devices

Some physical devices can move. We can write instructions to tell them where to go.

Once we have written our instructions, we can program the device.

Here is an example.

We want our physical device to follow this path through a grid.

To follow this path, we need to give the following instructions:

Algorithm 1

Step	Instruction
1	Move forward 1
2	Move forward 1
3	Move forward 1
4	Move forward 1
5	Turn right
6	Move forward 1
7	Move forward 1
8	Turn left
9	Move forward 1

Can you program your physical device to follow this path?

110

Some steps in Algorithm 1 are repeated.

We can rewrite the instructions like this:

Algorithm 2

Step	Instruction
1	Move forward 1
2	Repeat Step 1 three more times
3	Turn right
4	Move forward 1
5	Move forward 1
6	Turn left
7	Move forward 1

Algorithm 1 and Algorithm 2 do exactly the same thing.

There are 9 steps in Algorithm 1. There are only 7 steps in Algorithm 2.

Can your physical device repeat instructions? If it can, then program it to follow Algorithm 2.

Practise

Here is a path. We want our physical device to follow it.

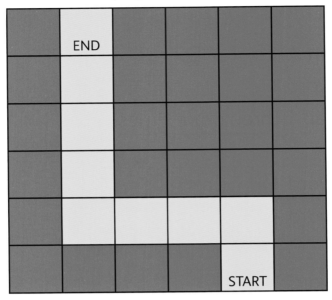

1   Here is the algorithm for this path.

Complete the blanks in the algorithm.

Algorithm 3

Step	Instruction
1	Move forward 1
2	Turn _____
3	Move forward 1
4	Move _____ 1
5	Move forward 1
6	Turn _____
7	Move _____ 1
8	_____
9	Move forward 1
10	_____

2   Work in small groups. Program your physical device to follow this path.

3   a   Rewrite Algorithm 3 using repeat instructions.

     b   How many steps does this new algorithm have?

4   If your physical device can repeat instructions, then program it to follow the algorithm in question **3 a**.

Go further

Computational thinking

1   See the steps below to draw the letter 'C' (⌐). Circle the correct answer in each step. Steps 1 and 2 are completed for you.

Step 1: (Start)/ Stop program

Step 2: Set marker up /(down)

Step 3: Turn left / right

Step 4: Move forward / backward by 8 cm

8 cm

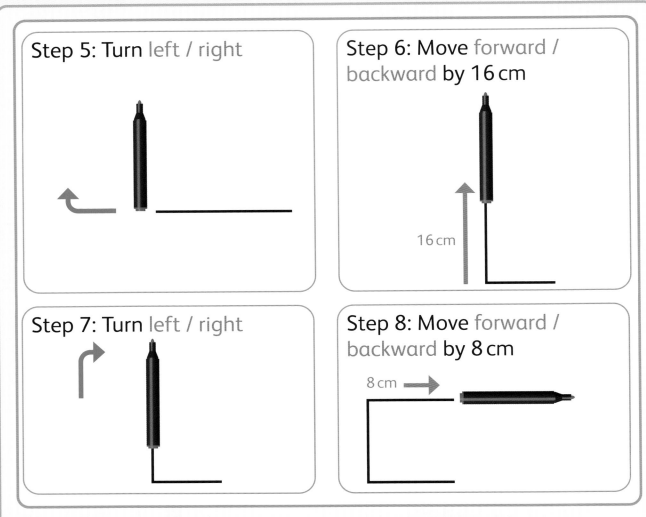

Step 5: Turn left / right

Step 6: Move forward / backward by 16 cm

16 cm

Step 7: Turn left / right

Step 8: Move forward / backward by 8 cm

8 cm

Below is a path through a grid. We want our physical device to follow it.

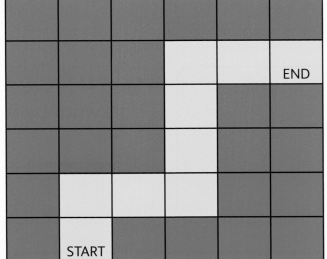

END

START

2 Here is the algorithm for this path. Complete the blanks in the algorithm.

Step	Instruction
①	Move _____
②	Turn _____
③	Move forward 1
④	Move _____ 1
⑤	Turn _____
⑥	_____
⑦	_____
⑧	Move forward 1
⑨	_____
⑩	Move forward 1
⑪	Move _____

3 Work in small groups. Program your physical device to follow this path.

4 a Rewrite the algorithm using repeat instructions.

   b How many steps does this new algorithm have?

5 If your physical device can repeat instructions, then program it to follow the Algorithm in question **3 a**.

⭐ Challenge yourself!

Computational thinking

1 Create the algorithm to draw the letter 'I'. Put the steps in the correct order. Steps 1, 2 and 3 are done for you.

Step ___: Move forward 8 cm

8 cm

Step **3**: Turn right

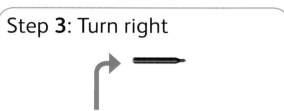

Step ___: Move forward 16 cm

16 cm

Step ___: Move backward 8 cm

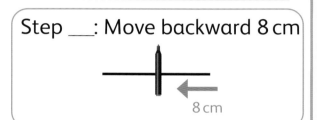

8 cm

Step ___: Move backward 16 cm

16 cm

Step ___: Turn left

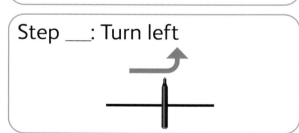

Step **1**: Start program

START

Step ___: Turn left

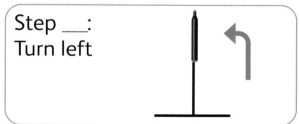

Step ___: Move forward 16 cm

16 cm

Step **2**: Set marker down

Below is a path through a grid.

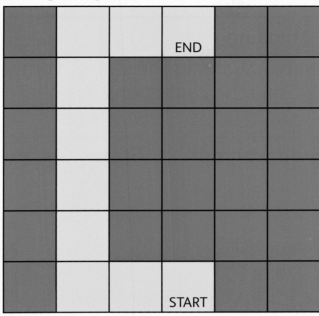

The path looks like the letter 'C'.

2 Write an algorithm to follow this path.

3 Program your physical device to follow this path, if you have one.

4 a Write a new algorithm for a path that looks like the number '0' (□).

   b If your device can draw, program it to draw the number '0'.

My project

Computational thinking

1   The algorithm below shows the steps to draw the letter 'P'. Circle the correct answer in each step.

Step 1: Start / Stop program

Step 2: Set marker up / down

Step 3: Move forward / backward by 16 cm

16 cm

Step 4: Turn left / right

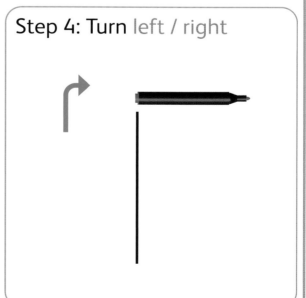

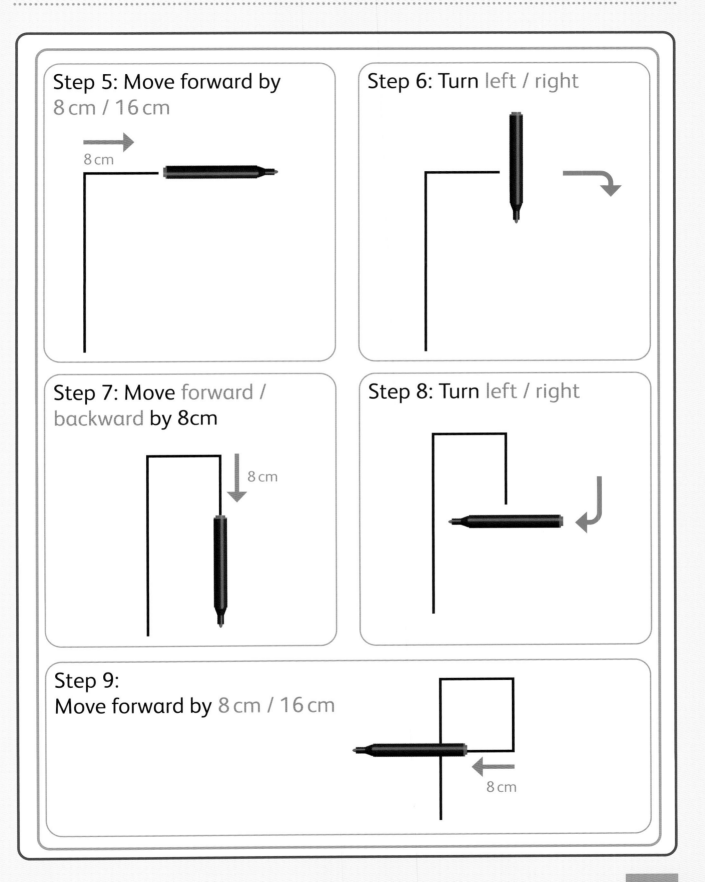

Step 5: Move forward by 8 cm / 16 cm

8 cm

Step 6: Turn left / right

Step 7: Move forward / backward by 8cm

8 cm

Step 8: Turn left / right

Step 9: Move forward by 8 cm / 16 cm

8 cm

Below is a path through a grid.

2   The algorithm below is for this path. There is one error in the algorithm. Find the error and rewrite the algorithm.

Step	Instruction
1	Move forward 1
2	Move forward 1
3	Turn right
4	Move forward 1
5	Move forward 1
6	Turn left
7	Move forward 1
8	Move forward 1
9	Turn left
10	Move forward 1
11	Move forward 1
12	Turn left
13	Move forward 1
14	Move forward 1
15	Move forward 1
16	Move forward 1
17	Move forward 1

3   Program your physical device to follow this path.

4   a   Rewrite the algorithm using repeat instructions.

    b   How many steps does this new algorithm have?

5   If your physical device can repeat instructions, then program it to follow the Algorithm in question **4 a**.

Notice that the shape of the path is the same as the letter 'P'.

Did you know?

You can code some physical devices to draw, play music, respond to touch, and more.

What can you do?

Read and review what you can do.

✔ I can write instructions to complete tasks.

✔ I can give directions to a physical device.

Great job! Now you know how to give direction instructions.

Connected and sharing

Networks

Get started!

Write your birthday on a sheet of paper.

Hand the paper to the person next to you.

Ask them to pass it to the person next to them.

The paper should not be folded.

- Is this a safe way to share information?
- How could you have kept your birthday secret?
- Could the person next to you see your birthday?

You will learn:

- to know when a network is and is not available
- about the risks of sharing information.

In this unit, you will learn about sharing information across networks.

Warm up

Talk about these questions with your partner.

- What is a network?
- What is the internet?
- How are networks connected?
- What devices can connect to a network?

Tell your partner what devices can do when they are connected to networks.

Do you remember?

Before starting this unit, check that you know that:

- some devices can connect to a network
- the internet is made of many computers connected together
- there are networks with and without wires
- there are times when the internet is not available.

Networks
Network availability

Learn

A device can connect to a network without wires.

The device shows this **icon**.

This tells you the device is connected without wires.

A device can connect to a network with a wire.

Some of the icons that show this include:

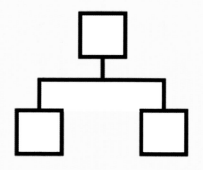 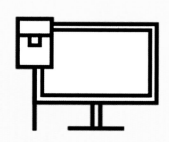 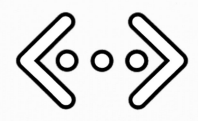

This tells you the device is connected with a wire.

The internet is made of lots of networks connected together.

Keyword
icon: a picture that means something on a computer

124

Devices show different icons when they are not connected to networks.

Smartphones and tablets show icons like this.

This means they are not connected.

Desktops and laptops show icons like this.

You cannot use the internet if you are not connected to a network. Devices may show messages to say you cannot use the internet.

The globe means the internet across the world. The circle with a line through shows the internet is not available.

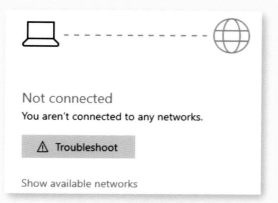

Not connected
You aren't connected to any networks.

⚠ Troubleshoot

Show available networks

Hmm. We're having trouble finding that site.

We can't connect to the server at www.google.com.

If that address is correct, here are three other things you can try:

• Try again later.
• Check your network connection.
• If you are connected but behind a firewall, check that Firefox has permission to access the Web.

Try Again

Connect to the internet

You're offline. Check your connection.

RETRY

If you cannot use the internet, then you cannot:
- send emails
- look at websites
- watch online videos.

Practise

1 a Which icon shows a device connected to a network by a wire?
    b Which icon shows a device connected to a network without a wire?

A    B    C

2 Select the icons that show there is no connection to a network.

A    B

C    D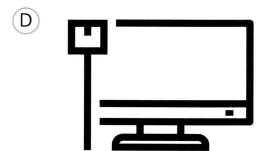

Sharing information across networks
The risks of sharing information

Learn

Devices on a network can share information with each other. This means data on one computer can be seen by another computer.

Connecting on a network has many benefits. However, there are also some risks. One of the largest risks is sharing personal information.

Personal information includes:

- address
- phone number
- family members' names
- birth date
- school names.

A device on a network sends information. Other people on the network may see it. This means that by sharing information on a network, other users may get your personal information.

Sharing personal information is one of the biggest risks of a network.

You send information when you:

- send emails
- enter details on websites
- send instant messages
- add things on social media.

> **Keyword**
> **personal information:** information about someone

Malware

Devices connected to a network also receive information. You receive information when you go to a website or download a file.

Programs that are bad for your computer are called **malware**. Some people try to trick you. They send malware across a network.

Signs that your device has malware:

- Your computer slows down.
- You get strange emails.
- You get strange adverts.
- Your device stops working.
- You cannot open your files.

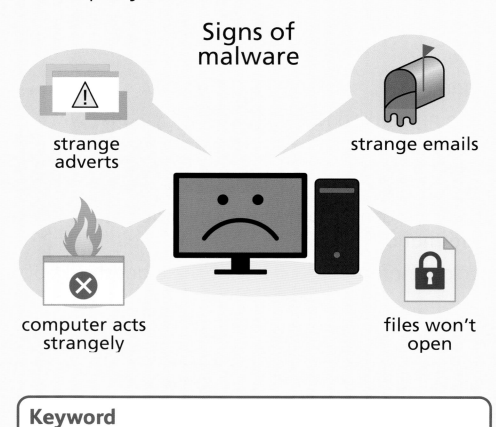

Signs of malware

strange adverts

strange emails

computer acts strangely

files won't open

> **Keyword**
> **malware:** a program that is bad for a computer

Stay Safe

Do not give out your personal information to people/places you do not know.

Accepting Files

Accepting emails, files, pictures or texts from people you do not know can cause problems.

Tell Someone

Tell an adult if someone or something makes you feel worried or uncomfortable.

Follow these SMART tips to keep yourself safe online!

Don't Meet Up

Meeting someone online can be dangerous. Always check with an adult you trust.

Reliable?

Check information before you believe it. Is the person or website telling the truth?

Computer scientists have ways to protect your information and computer devices. You will learn about these in Stage 6!

Practise

1   Tick (✔) true or false.

Statement	True	False
a Data on one computer can be seen by a computer on the network.		
b Sharing personal information is not safe.		
c One of the biggest online risks is the sharing of personal information.		

2   Copy the sentences. Fill in the blank space with the correct word(s). Words can be used more than once.

(emails)   (address)   (malware)

a   If you download _____, your computer acts strangely.

b   Your _____ is an example of personal information.

c   You share information when you send _____.

d   _____ can cause harm to your computer.

Go further

1   Tick (✔) the statements that are true.

   a   Sharing information on a network has benefits.

   b   Devices connected to a network cannot share information stored on the individual computers with each other.

   c   Sharing information on a network can cause harm to the data stored on your computer.

d   Sharing information on a network cannot put the computer at risk. ☐

e   Once people who do not have permission have seen your data, it is easy to know how many people have looked at it. ☐

2   Draw an icon for a device connected to a network with wires.

3   Draw an icon for a device connected to a network without wires.

4   How can people without permission see personal information?

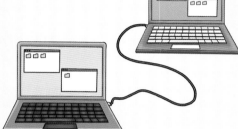

Challenge yourself!

1   Draw one icon to show the internet is available on a device.

2   Draw one icon to show the internet is not available on a device.

3   Point to the pictures that show personal information.

My home address

My phone number

My date of birth

My robot toy

My bicycle

4   Tell your partner one more example of personal information.

My project

1   Create a flyer that shows what information can be shared on the internet. Which devices might you use to share that information? Choose the correct pictures from those shown below to add to the flyer.

Sending emails

Making a phone call

Entering information on a website

Sending instant messages

Posting a letter

Chatting with a friend on social media

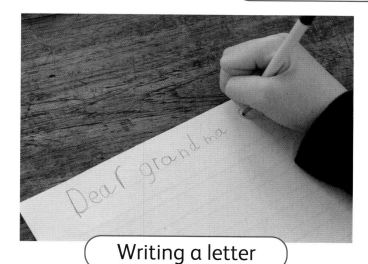

Writing a letter

2   Draw a poster to show that a computer may have malware. Tell your partner what malware is and what the poster is showing.

What can you do?

Read and review what you can do.
   ✔ I know when a network is and is not available.
   ✔ I know about the risks of sharing information.

Great job! Now you know about icons and the risks with networks.

Creating stories

Get started!

Work in pairs. Tell your partner what you think this story is about.

You will learn:

- to predict what algorithms do
- to regularly test programs while writing them
- to debug programs.

In this unit, you will test and debug programs.

Warm up

Look at the path the sailor takes to the treasure.

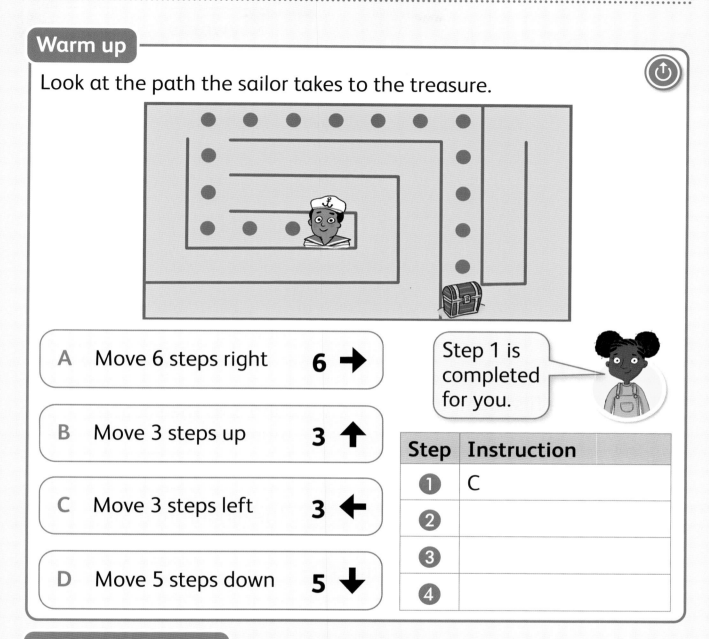

A	Move 6 steps right	6 ➡
B	Move 3 steps up	3 ⬆
C	Move 3 steps left	3 ⬅
D	Move 5 steps down	5 ⬇

Step 1 is completed for you.

Step	Instruction	
1	C	
2		
3		
4		

Do you remember?

Before starting this unit, check that you can:
- create algorithms as programs
- plan the instructions for characters within programs.

In this unit, you will use ScratchJr.
There is an online chapter all about ScratchJr.

Input and output
Predicting algorithm output

Keywords
output: the results of an algorithm
input: the data that is given to an algorithm

Learn

To predict the **output** of an algorithm, we must:
- **input** data
- carry out each instruction in the algorithm.

Look at the algorithm below. It adds two numbers and then shows the total.

1 Start program

2 Enter the first number

3 Enter the second number

4 Add the first and second numbers

5 Show the answer

6 Stop program

If we enter 5 as the first number

5

and 3 as the second number

3

the algorithm adds 5 and 3

5 + 3

which is 8.

8

The output is 8.

We work through the steps of the algorithm, using the data, just as the computer would.

Practise

Look at these two algorithms.

Predict the output of each algorithm if we input the number **4** for both.

Compare your answers with your partner.

Algorithm A

1. Start program
2. Enter a number
3. Add 3
4. Multiply by 2
5. Subtract the number by 4
6. Multiply by 2
7. Add 5
8. Show final number
9. Stop program

Algorithm B

1. Start program
2. Enter a number
3. Subtract 1
4. Multiply by 2
5. Add 2
6. Multiply by 2
7. Subtract 2
8. Show final number
9. Stop program

Testing programs

Programs should be tested while we write them.

By testing programs while writing them, we can:
- keep checking the results are correct
- test smaller groups of code
- stop errors being repeated.

Example of testing a program regularly
This algorithm is for the **Person** character. The algorithm has two parts. Part 1 is shown below.

Part 1	
1	Start on Green Flag
2	Say "Hi, welcome!"
3	Say "My name is Mr Williams."
4	Send Orange Start Message
5	Stop program

We can create the code for Part 1 and test it.

The code for Part 1 is shown below.

We can test this code by tapping the **Start on Green Flag** block.

We find an error. The second block does not match Step 2.

We correct the **second** block as seen below.

Part 2	
①	Start on Red Message
②	Say "Hi nice to meet you."
③	Send Blue Start Message
④	Stop program

Since we have corrected the error now, we will have fewer errors to fix at the end!

The algorithm for Part 2 is shown above. The code for this algorithm is:

We can test this code by tapping the **Start on Red Message** block.

It matches the algorithm and has no errors.

When we test the whole program, there are no errors. This is because we have already tested Parts 1 and 2 separately.

Practise

1 Open a new project and add any Background.
2 Add a **Child** character.
3 Add code to match the Part 3 algorithm and test it.

Part 3	
①	Start on Orange Message
②	Say "Hi, my name is Mary."
③	Send Red Start Message
④	Stop program

4 Add code to a second character to match the Part 4 algorithm and test it.

Part 4	
①	Start on Blue Message
②	Say "Nice to meet you too."
③	Jump (2)
④	Stop program

5 Test the whole program to make sure it works correctly.

You tested the program as you created it, so it is more likely that the whole program is correct.

Debugging programs

Learn

Programs may have errors if they are not written correctly.

We debug programs so that they give the results we want.

To debug a program, we need to find which part of the code does not give the correct result.

Look at this algorithm and program created for a **Person** character.

Step	Instruction
1	Start on Green Flag
2	Move right (3)
3	Say "Hi, how are you?"
4	Send Green Start Message
5	Stop program

If you compare the algorithm to the program, you should notice that this code has two errors.

We can change the two blocks that contain errors. Now the code matches the algorithm.

- We changed **4** to **3** in the **Move Right** block.
- We changed the **Send Orange Start Message** block to the **Send Green Start Message** block.

Practise

In this activity, you will practice debugging by yourself!

1 Open a new project and add any Background.

2 Add a **Person** character.

3 Add the correct code for the algorithm on the previous page.

4 Add another **Person** character.

Look at the algorithm below for the second **Person** character.

Step	Instruction
①	Start on Green Message
②	Move left (2)
③	Say "Hi, I'm great!"
④	Say "How about you?"
⑤	Stop program

Hi, I'm great!

5 Add the code below to the second **Person** character.

6 Debug the code above.

7 Add more code to the second **Person** character to match the algorithm below.

Step	Instruction
①	Start on Green Flag
②	Turn Right (1)
③	Jump (2)
④	Turn Left (1)
⑤	Stop program

Remember to test your code as you create your program.

8 Test and debug the whole program.

9 Compare your program with your partner.

Go further

Computational thinking

1   What is the output of this algorithm if 10 is the input?

Step	Instruction
❶	Start program
❷	Enter a number
❸	Subtract 4
❹	Show final number
❺	Stop program

2   Open a new project and add any Background.

3   Add a **Child** character (Child 1). Create a program to match the Child 1 algorithm.

Child 1 Character	
❶	Start on Green Flag
❷	Say "Have you been using my crayons?"
❸	Send Blue Start Message
❹	Stop program

4   Test and debug the **Child 1** code.

5   Add another **Child** character (Child 2) to your project.

Child 2 Character	
①	Start on Blue Message
②	Say "No, I have not."
③	Stop program

6   Add the code below to **Child 2**.

7   Test and debug the **Child 2** code.

8   Run, test and debug your complete program.

⭐ Challenge yourself!

Continue the program from the **Go further** activity as follows.

1 Add a second page to your project. (Your teacher can help you.)

2 Add this code to the **Child 1** character on the first page:

> Can you guess what this code means?

3 Add the same **Child 1** character as before to the second page.

4 Add a third **Child** character (Child 3) to the second page.

5 Add code to the characters to match the algorithms below.

Page 2: Child 1 Character	
❶	Start on Tap
❷	Say "Have you been using my crayons?"
❸	Send Red Start Message
❹	Stop program

Page 2: Child 3 Character	
❶	Start on Red Message
❷	Say "Yes, I used them yesterday to draw."
❸	Jump (2)
❹	Stop program

6 Test and debug your code while writing it.

Your program should look something like this:

Page 1

Page 2

My project

1 What is the output of the algorithm below if the input number is 3?

Step	Instruction
1	Start program
2	Enter a number
3	Multiply the number by 2
4	Show final number
5	Stop program

2 Open a new project with 2 pages.

3 Add a **Penguin** character to Page 1. Create a program to match the algorithm below.

Page 1: Penguin Character
1	Start on Green Flag
2	Move left (8)
3	Go to Page 2

4 Test and debug your code.

5 Add a **Penguin** and **Polar Bear** character to Page 2.

6 Add the code below to the **Polar Bear** character.

7   Debug the code you added to match the algorithm below.

Page 2: Polar Bear Character	
❶	Start on Tap
❷	Move right (1)
❸	Play pop sound
❹	Say "Hi, Mr Penguin."
❺	Jump (2)
❻	Stop program

Test your code regularly while you create your program.

Did you know?

The first electronic digital computer could run different programs. It was operated by six women.

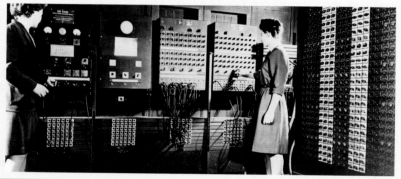

What can you do?

Read and review what you can do.

✔ I can predict what algorithms do.

✔ I know why I should regularly test programs while writing them.

✔ I can debug programs.

Good job! Now you can test and debug programs.

Computers and robots

Who is quicker?

Get started!

Talk about the following with a partner:

Your friend adds two numbers together without using a calculator. You add the same numbers using a calculator.

Who would get the answer first?

Now imagine there are ten numbers to add together. Who would get the answer first?

You will learn:

- about tasks computers can do better than humans
- that people use different types of computer devices
- about robots in fiction and real robots.

In this unit, you will learn about things robots and computers can do.

Warm up

Work in groups.

  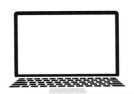

Help Gina name the different types of computers shown above.

Name two jobs shown in the picture below.

Discuss with your partner if you think people use computers in these jobs. What do they use them for?

Do you remember?

Before starting this unit, check that you:

- can explain what basic hardware and software can do
- know computers are used for different things
- know what a robot is and where they may be found.

Computers and humans

Learn

Computers can do some things better than humans.

Computers can perform tasks for a long time

Computers do not get tired. Computers do not get bored. They do not need to take a break.

Computers store a lot of information

Computers can store lots of information in a small space.

A single computer can store a whole library of books!

Computers do as they are told

Computers follow instructions. They do not make mistakes. Mistakes are due to humans.

Computers are fast

Computers are very fast. They can perform millions of tasks every second.

They can add numbers much quicker than humans.

Practise

1 A teacher marks tests for the whole school. She has to remember each student's score.

   a Do you think a computer is better at marking tests?

   b Do you think a computer is better at remembering scores?

2 Sara tries to build a doll house. However, she does not follow the instructions. The doll house falls apart. What went wrong? Tick (✔) the correct answer.

   • There was an error in the instructions. ☐
   • The instructions were not followed. ☐

3 Billy believes he can draw a house faster than a computer. Is Billy right?

4 Work in groups of four. Explain three things that computers can do better than humans.

Choosing computer devices

Learn

People choose computer devices for different reasons.

Their location

If someone sits at a desk for many hours each day, they may prefer a desktop computer.

A desktop is larger, heavier and not easy to move.

Laptops, tablets and smartphones are smaller, lighter and easy to move. If someone is moving around, they may prefer these portable devices.

Smartphones can connect to the internet anywhere.

The purpose

The choice of device depends on what it is being used for.

A delivery driver uses a tablet.

A tablet is easier to carry than a laptop. It has a bigger screen than a smartphone.

A graphic designer needs a powerful computer. They use a desktop computer as they are more powerful. They have large screens.

Attaching other devices

Sometimes people need to attach devices to their computer. A laptop or desktop can connect to a mouse and keyboard.

However, a smartphone cannot connect to these devices.

Battery

How long does the battery last?

- Laptops – will need recharging more than once a day.
- Tablets – will need recharging once a day.
- Smartphones – can last more than a day before recharging.

Practise

Discuss the following with your partner.

1   Annay's brother needs a new computer device.
    He needs a device that:

    •   is light and easy to carry around

    •   has a long battery life.

    Point to the device you would choose for him.

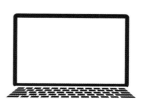

2   Jin's sister takes photographs. She needs to connect a
    digital camera and printer. She needs a computer to
    connect to the camera and to print out images.

    Point to the device you would choose for her.

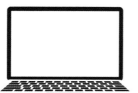

3   Some devices are easier to move than others. Arrange the devices below from easiest to carry to hardest to carry.

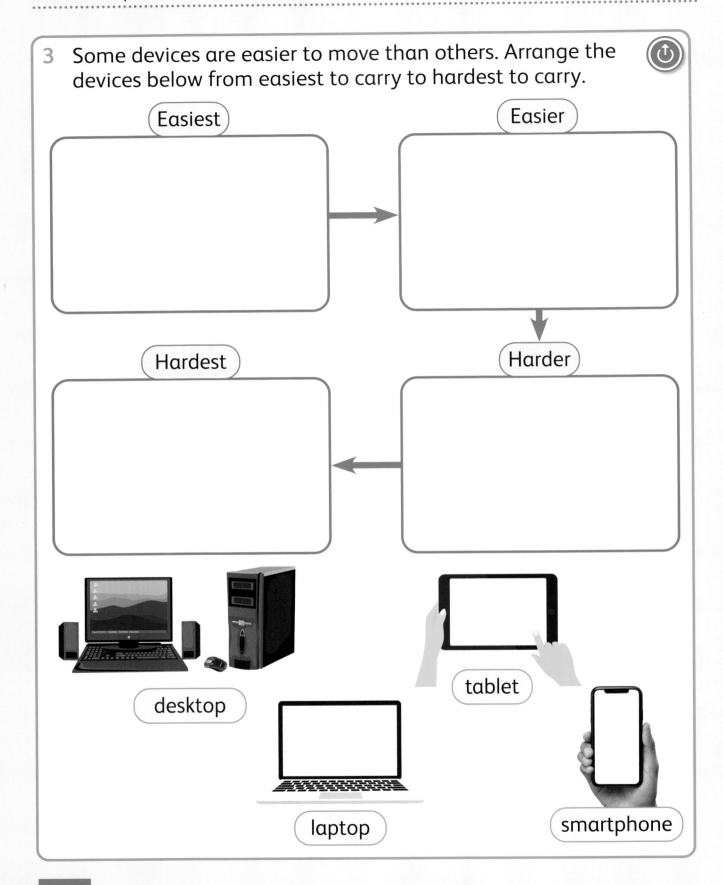

Easiest

Easier

Hardest

Harder

desktop

tablet

laptop

smartphone

Robots: real or fictional?

Do you remember what a **robot** is?

A robot is a machine that can do a task without any help.

You may have seen robots in movies.

Robots in movies are not real. Things that are not real are called **fictional**.

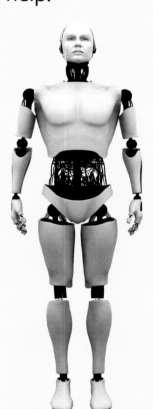

Fictional robots often:
- look like humans
- speak like humans
- act a bit like humans.

This picture shows a fictional robot. This robot does not really exist.

Real robots:
- do not always look like humans
- may not speak at all
- repeat the same tasks or actions
- do not act like humans.

Some examples of real robots are shown below.
These robots are found in factories.

This robot cuts grass.

Keywords

robot: a machine that does a task without the help of a person

fictional: not real – make believe

Practise

1 Say if the following statements are true or false.

Statement	True or false?
a A robot can feel sad.	
b A robot can go into space.	
c Robots cannot do dangerous work.	
d A real robot can make cars.	
e All robots look like humans.	

2 After watching a movie on television, Vicki believed that all robots are real.

a Explain to Vicki that some robots are fictional while some are real.

b Give some examples of the differences between real and fictional robots.

3 With a partner, choose one of the robots shown and say whether it is fictional or real. Explain your answer.

Go further

1   Jessie uses a broom to clean. Dana says that a robot vacuum cleaner can do a better job. Do you think she is correct? Explain your answer.

2   Danny uses his computer to design things.

    Work in groups. Which device do you think Danny should use? Explain why you chose that device.

3   Do these robots look real or fictional? Give a reason for your answer.

Challenge yourself!

Work with a partner.

1 What is a fictional robot?

2 Can you name two robots in movies that are fictional?

3 Jon and Jeff are searching for information. Jon uses a search engine on a computer. Jeff goes to the library and looks for books.

    a Who will find information first?

    b Who will find more information?

4 Anton travels for work. Pedro works in his office. Anton uses a laptop.

    a Why do you think Anton chose a laptop? Choose two reasons from this list:

       (A laptop is heavy.)   (A laptop is easy to move.)

       (A laptop screen is bigger than a tablet.)

       (Anton does not need a keyboard.)

    b Which type of computer should Pedro use? Explain why.

My project

Work with a partner:

1 Look at the pictures below. Both the human and the robot are working underwater.
    a Is the job more dangerous for the human or the robot?
    b Do you think the robot is real or fictional?

2 a Which of these jobs would be safer for a robot to do?

Clean windows on a skyscraper ◯   Cut the grass ◯

Tidy a classroom ◯

  b Which of these tasks are easier for a computer to do than a human?

Count the number of words in a book ◯   Write a joke ◯

Remember all the results of a class test ◯

3 There are two tasks shown on the next page. For each task, say whether you think people or robots would do a faster job. Give a reason for your answer.

Task 1

People making a car.

Robot arms making a car.

Task 2

A person checking drink bottles in a factory.

Robots checking drink bottles in a factory.

What can you do?

Read and review what you can do.

✔ I know about tasks computers can do better than humans.

✔ I know that people choose different computer devices for different reasons.

✔ I know the difference between fictional and real robots.

Great job! Now you know a bit more about fictional and real robots.

Glossary

A

app: a program that performs a task

B

backup: a copy of data that is stored in a safe place

barcode: black lines that contain information about an item

bug: a mistake in an algorithm or program

C

category: group
code: the instructions in a program

D

debug: to find and remove errors in a program

E

edit: to make changes or corrections

F

fictional: not real – make believe

function: the things that a device can do

H

hardware: physical objects that make up a computer

I

icon: a picture that means something on a computer

input: the data that is given to an algorithm

input device: hardware that puts data into a digital device

M

malware: a program that is bad for a computer

O

output: the results of an algorithm

output device: hardware that lets us hear or see information

P

personal information: information about someone

portable: easy to carry

precise: exact, clear and correct

present: to show

program: a set of instructions for a computer

R

repeat: do something again

robot: a machine that does a task without the help of a person

S

software: a set of instructions for a computer

U

user-friendly: how easy something is to use

Acknowledgements

The Publishers would like to thank the following for permission to reproduce copyright material. Every effort has been made to trace or contact all copyright holders, but if any have been inadvertently overlooked, the Publishers will be pleased to make the necessary arrangements at the first opportunity.

Text acknowledgements
pp. 4, 6–7, 9, 11–23, 55, 60–64, 80–81, 84–91, 135, 138–147 © Scratch is developed by the Lifelong Kindergarten Group at the MIT Media Lab. See http://scratch.mit.edu. Licensed under a Creative Commons Attribution-ShareAlike 2.0 Generic license (CC BY-SA 2.0).

Photo acknowledgements
p. 5 *cl*, **p. 42** *cc*, **p. 45** *cc* © Angkhan/Adobe Stock Photo; **pp. 6 –7, 11–23, 60–64, 84–91, 140–148** © Scratch is developed by the Lifelong Kindergarten Group at the MIT Media Lab. See http://scratch.mit.edu. Licensed under a Creative Commons Attribution-ShareAlike 2.0 Generic license (CC BY-SA 2.0); **p. 10** *cr* © Igor Photo 50/Adobe Stock Photo; **p. 24** *cc* © Ольга Погорелова/Adobe Stock Photo; **p. 27** *br* © Sensay/Adobe Stock Photo; **pp. 29–30, 37** *br* © 2021 MathsIsFun.com; **p. 35** *tl* © Samadan/Adobe Stock Photo; **p. 35** *tc* © Yeti Studio/Adobe Stock Photo; **p. 35** *tc* © Comicsans/Adobe Stock Photo; **p. 35** *tc* © Scanrail/Adobe Stock Photo; **p. 35** *tr* © Tabor Chichakly/Adobe Stock Photo; **p. 35** *cc*, **p. 41** *cr*, **p. 51** *cl* © Maksim Masalski/Adobe Stock Photo; **p. 35** *cc* © Vchalup/Adobe Stock Photo; **p. 35** *bc*, **p. 45** *cc*, **p. 49** *cr*, **p. 51** *cr*, **p. 164** *tr* © Techstock Studio/Adobe Stock Photo; **p. 41** *cl*, **p. 49** *cc*, **p. 50** *cr*, **p. 51** *cl* © New Africa/Adobe Stock Photo; **p. 41** *cc*, **p. 45** *cc* © Rahmawati Dian/Adobe Stock Photo; **p. 41** *cr*, **p. 151** *cc*, **p. 156** *cl, cc*, **p. 157** *br*, **p. 161** *cc* © Amenic 181/Adobe Stock Photo; **p. 41** *cl*, **p. 151** *cc*, **p. 156** *cr, cc*, **p. 157** *cc*, **p. 161** *cc* © Anatolii/Adobe Stock Photo; **p. 41** *cc* © Used with permission from Ningbo Jus Internet Technology Co. Ltd.; **p. 41** *cc*, **p. 49** *cl*, **p. 50** *cl*, **p. 51** *cr* © Irina/Adobe Stock Photo; **p. 41** *cr* © Ion Popa/Adobe Stock Photo; **p. 41** *cl*, **p. 49** *cc*, **p. 50** *cl*, **p. 51** *ibl* © Foto Fabrika/Adobe Stock Photo; **p. 41** *cc* Zoom and the Zoom logo are trademarks of Zoom Video Communications, Inc.; **p. 45** *cc*, **p. 47** *cr* © MMG1 Design/Adobe Stock Photo; **p. 45** *cc*, **p. 49** *cc*, **p. 50** *cc*, **p. 51** *cc*, **p. 164** *br* © Artem Merzlenko/Adobe Stock Photo; **p. 46** *cr* © Nirutft/Adobe Stock Photo; **p. 46** *br* © LightField Studios Inc/Adobe Stock Photo; **p. 47** *tr* © Mclittle Stock/Adobe Stock Photo; **p. 47** *bl* © Scanrail/Adobe Stock Photo; **p. 49** *cr*, **p. 50** *cc*, **p. 51** *cc* © Premkh/Adobe Stock Photo; **p. 49** *cl* © Alexandr Chubarov/Adobe Stock Photo; **p. 49** *cc*, **p. 50** *cc* © Destina/Adobe Stock Photo; **p. 49** *cr*, **p. 68** *cr*, **p. 70** *tc* © Stock Photos Art/Adobe Stock Photo; **p. 49** *cl*, **p. 50** *cr*, **p. 51** *cl* © Goir/Adobe Stock Photo; **p. 50** *cc* © Andrey Zyk/Adobe Stock Photo; **p. 51** *bc* © Naravit/Adobe Stock Photo; **p. 51** *br* © Andregric/Adobe Stock Photo; **p. 54** *cl* © Andre D/Adobe Stock Photo; **p. 54** *cc* © Ljupco Smokovski/Adobe Stock Photo; **p. 54** *cr* © Subbotina Anna/Adobe Stock Photo; **p. 54** *cl* © A Skorobogatova/Adobe Stock Photo; **p. 54** *cc* © Nnui 2527/Adobe Stock Photo; **p. 54** *cr* © Dmytro Flisak/Adobe Stock Photo; **p. 58** *tr* © Africa Studio/Adobe Stock Photo; **p. 65** *cc* © Reuters/Alamy Stock Photo; **p. 66** *cl* © Shotshop GmbH/Alamy Stock Photo; **p. 66** *cr* © Miri García/Adobe Stock Photo; **p. 68** *cr*, **p. 70** *tl* © Slay Storm/Adobe Stock Photo; **p. 68** *br*, **p. 70** *tr, br* © Tiler 84/Adobe Stock Photo; **p. 69** *tr* © Can Be Done/Adobe Stock Photo; **p. 69** *cr* © Nor Gal/Adobe Stock Photo; **p. 69** *cr* © RH2010/Adobe Stock Photo; **p. 69** *br* © Phonlamai Photo/Adobe Stock Photo; **p. 70** *bl* © Dzm1try/Adobe Stock Photo; **p. 70** *bc* © Blueee/Adobe Stock Photo; **p. 70** *bc* © Nat/Adobe Stock Photo; **p. 82** *cr* © Passiflora 70/Adobe Stock Photo; **p. 108** *cc*, **p. 109** *cc*, **p. 113** *cc*, **p. 114** *cc*, **p. 116** *cc*, **p. 118** *cc*, **p. 119** *cc* © Kup 1984/Adobe Stock Photo; **p. 122** *cc* © Lightfield Studios/Adobe Stock Photo; **p. 125** *cc* © Ferhad/Adobe Stock Photo; **p. 125** *cc* © Pixxsa/Adobe Stock Photo; **p. 125** *br, bl* © Google™ search is a trademark of Google LLC. Google and Google Docs are trademarks of Google LLC and this book is not endorsed by or affiliated with Google in any way; **p. 125** *bc* © Used with permission from Microsoft; **p. 131** *cl* © Cosveta/Adobe Stock Photo; **p. 131** *cc* © Anya/Adobe Stock Photo; **p. 131** *cc* © J Funk/Adobe Stock Photo; **p. 131** *cc* © Vladislav Ociacia/Adobe Stock Photo; **p. 131** *cr* © Stockphoto-Graf/Adobe Stock Photo; **p. 132** *cc* © Hanss/Adobe Stock Photo; **p. 132** *cl* © Studio Grand Web/Adobe Stock Photo; **p. 132** *bc* © Mykyta/Adobe Stock Photo; **p. 133** *cl* © Matthew Ashmore/Adobe Stock Photo; **p. 133** *cr* © Redpixel/Adobe Stock Photo; **p. 133** *cc* © Rocklights/Adobe Stock Photo; **p. 148** *cc* © Bettmann/Contributor/Getty Images; **p. 149** *cc* © Kanpitcha Nonnittayanan/Eye Em/Adobe Stock Photo; **p. 150** *cl*, **p. 156** *cc, cl*, **p. 157** *bc*, **p. 161** *cl* © Prostoira 777/Adobe Stock Photo; **p. 150** *cr*, **p. 152** *br*, **p. 156** *cc, br*, **p. 157** *cl*, **p. 161** *cr* © Javid Kheyrabadi/Adobe Stock Photo; **p. 150** *cc* © Ivan Mogilevchik/Adobe Stock Photo; **p. 151** *cc* © Charnsitr/Adobe Stock Photo; **p. 153** *tr* © Rocket Clips/Adobe Stock Photo; **p. 153** *cr* © Merla/Adobe Stock Photo; **p. 153** *br* © Syda Productions/Adobe Stock Photo; **p. 154** *cc* © Andrey Popov/Adobe Stock Photo; **p. 154** *cc* © Saiful Alam/Alamy Stock Photo; **p. 154** *br* © Fotobieshutterb/Adobe Stock Photo; **p. 157** *cc* © Epix Productions/Adobe Stock Photo; **p. 157** *cr* © Sarah Holmlund/Adobe Stock Photo; **p. 158** *cc* © Ipopba/Adobe Stock Photo; **p. 158** *cc* © Molpix/Shutterstock.com; **p. 158** *bc*, **p. 165** *cr* © Ureschke/Adobe Stock Photo; **p. 159** *bl* © Tetsuya Nemoto/Adobe Stock Photo; **p. 159** *br*, **p. 165** *cl* © Phonlamai Photo/Adobe Stock Photo; **p. 160** *bc* © Phonlamai Photo/Adobe Stock Photo; **p. 163** *tl* © Everettovrk/Adobe Stock Photo; **p. 163** *tr* © Think A/Shutterstock.com; **p. 163** *cl* © Nikomsolftwaer/Adobe Stock Photo; **p. 163** *cr* © Industrieblick/Adobe Stock Photo.

t = top, *b* = bottom, *l* = left, *r* = right, *c* = centre